Forthcoming Volumes in the Philosophy A–Z Series

Chinese Philosophy A–Z, Bo Mou
Christian Philosophy A–Z, Daniel Hill
Ethics A–Z, Jon Jacobs
Feminist Philosophy A–Z, Nancy McHugh
Indian Philosophy A–Z, Christopher Bartley
Islamic Philosophy A–Z, Peter Groff
Jewish Philosophy A–Z, Aaron Hughes
Metaphysics A–Z, Peter Groff
Philosophical Logic A–Z, J. C. Beall
Philosophy of Language A–Z, Allessandro Tanesini
Philosophy of Law and Legal Theory A–Z, Patrick O'Donnell
Philosophy of Mind A–Z, Marina Rakova
Philosophy of Religion A–Z, Patrick Quinn
Philosophy of Science A–Z, Stathis Psillos

Epistemology A–Z

Martijn Blaauw
and
Duncan Pritchard

Edinburgh University Press

© Martijn Blaauw and Duncan Pritchard, 2005

Edinburgh University Press Ltd
22 George Square, Edinburgh

Typeset in 10.5/13 Sabon
by TechBooks India, and printed and
bound in Finland by WS Bookwell

A CIP record for this book is
available from the British Library

ISBN 0 7486 2213 6 (hardback)
ISBN 0 7486 2094 X (paperback)

The right of Martijn Blaauw and Duncan Pritchard
to be identified as authors of this work
has been asserted in accordance with
the Copyright, Designs and Patents Act 1988.

Contents

Series Editor's Preface

One of the primary topics in philosophy deals with the theory of knowledge, and in particular the issue of what we can know. Almost all philosophers have addressed themselves to the topic, which might be said to define what philosophy is all about. After all, the desire to philosophise in the first place is often a matter of wondering what sorts of knowledge are available to us. The theory of knowledge or epistemology has blossomed into a vast set of theories and concepts that look at all aspects of the issue of what sorts of knowledge are available to us. The authors of this book have presented a comprehensive guide to the main ideas and thinkers that readers will come across in the literature, and they have brought out the links that exist between these ideas and thinkers. Some epistemological concepts are highly technical in their scope, yet they all stem from quite clear and familiar notions, and the language of the text attempts to replicate this. One of the familiar reactions of those coming to philosophy for the first time is that we are not justified in thinking that we know what we clearly in ordinary language terms do know, and it is in trying to resolve that issue that so much of the theory of knowledge gets going. The authors take us a fair way along this route, and explore what branches off it. Since the distinctions between the different theoretical positions in the area are often rather fine, there is a need for precision in describing those positions. The result is that the reader should be able to gain a clear view of the scope of epistemological questions, and so indeed very much of philosophy as a whole.

Oliver Leaman

Introduction and Acknowledgements

Epistemology is one of the oldest branches of philosophy. This is unsurprising once one reflects that it is also one of the most *important* branches of philosophy because its object of study – human knowledge – plays such a vital role in our lives. Philosophy without epistemology would not be philosophy.

This dictionary aims to introduce the reader to the main epistemological positions and figures. In order to achieve this, we have tried to make each entry as precise and concise as possible. In addition, each entry is cross-referenced so that the reader will acquire a multi-layered view of the debates that she is interested in. Finally, each entry is followed by a short bibliography which cites the main texts that we recommend reading if readers wish to pursue a particular subject beyond the bounds of this dictionary.

We would like to thank the staff at Edinburgh University Press for having made the writing of this dictionary such a pleasurable experience. In particular, we would like to thank Oliver Leaman, Jackie Jones, Nicola Wood and Anna Somerville for their editorial support. Finally, Martijn wishes to thank the Niels Stensen foundation for the financial support that made writing this dictionary possible, and the Department of Philosophy at the University of Aarhus where part of this dictionary was written.

Aarhus, Denmark/Stirling, Scotland
March 2005

Epistemology A–Z

A

Abductive reasoning: Abductive reasoning – also known as inference to the best **explanation** or hypothetical **induction** – is a variety of induction. Like all forms of inductive inference, it is non-deductive, but unlike enumerative induction where a generalisation is inferred from a suitable set of instances of that generalisation, abduction is where a hypothesis is inferred as the best explanation of the available **evidence**. For example, the best explanation of the dent in one's car bonnet could be that the teenagers hanging around nearby have caused it. Note, however, that this inference is not normally understood as resting upon one's observation of a correlation between the presence of teenagers and vandalism to one's car (as would be the case in an enumerative inductive inference), and so the inference in question is not obviously reducible to an enumerative inductive inference. **DHP**

See **deduction; explanation; induction**

Further reading: Lipton 1991

Ability knowledge: It is common in **epistemology** to make a distinction between at least three types of **knowledge**: **propositional knowledge** (or 'knowing that'), **interrogative knowledge** (or 'knowing why/what/where/when/

which/whether/who'), and ability knowledge (or 'knowing how'). Examples of the last type of knowledge would be 'knowing how to ride a bicycle', or 'knowing how to cook dinner'. An important controversy in the epistemological literature concerns the relationship between 'knowing how' and 'knowing that'. One important view, put forward by **Ryle**, has it that 'knowing how' and 'knowing that' are completely different: 'knowing how' is an ability, whereas 'knowing that' is a relation between a subject and a **proposition**. This view is held to be problematic for various reasons, if only because there is a clear sense in which some 'knowing how' expressions have nothing to do with abilities (consider, for instance, 'I know how the butler was murdered'). Ryle's view has recently been challenged by Stanley and **Williamson**, who argue that 'knowing how' reduces to 'knowing that'. **MB**

See **interrogative knowledge; propositional knowledge; Ryle, Gilbert; Williamson, Timothy**

Further reading: Ryle 1949; Stanley and Williamson 2001

Absolute term: According to **Unger**, some terms in a language (for instance, 'flat' and 'empty') are absolute terms. Absolute terms indicate an absolute limit which can hardly ever be reached. For a table to be flat, for instance, it should have no bumps or irregularities *at all*. Now Unger argued that **knowledge** is an absolute term as well. More specifically, he argued that knowledge implies **certainty**, and that certainty is an absolute term, since one is only certain of a **belief** when the belief in question is infallible. But since not many of our beliefs are infallible, it follows that we are rarely properly certain of anything and thus that we rarely know anything. **MB**

See **certainty; infallibilism; infallibility; scepticism; Unger, Peter**

Further reading: Lewis 1996; Schaffer 2005b; Unger 1975

Acceptance: It does not follow from the fact that one believes a **proposition** that one will always assent to that proposition if called upon to do so, or that one would only assent to propositions that one believes. There are a number of reasons for this, including insincerity, self-deceit and lack of confidence in what one believes. When one accepts a proposition one is willing to assent to it, and, given the foregoing, acceptance thereby picks out a different notion from **belief. DHP**
See **belief**
Further reading: Cohen 1992; Lehrer 1990b

Acquaintance knowledge: see **knowledge by acquaintance**

Adverbial theories: Adverbial theories of **experience** rephrase descriptions of experience in terms of a complex adverb, as in the following case, where (1) is redescribed as (2):

1. John is experiencing a blue triangle.
2. John is experiencing (blue triangle)-ly.

The advantage of employing this redescription is that the truth of (1) seems to require the existence of the relevant object, in this case the blue triangle. In contrast, (2) makes no such demand. Adverbial theories are thus useful if one wishes to offer an account of experience which is not object-involving. **DHP**
See **experience; perception**
Further reading: Chisholm 1957

Agent reliabilism: see **reliabilism**

Agrippa's trilemma: Agrippa was an advocate of **Pyrrhonian scepticism,** who probably lived sometime around the first century AD. He argued that, faced with a challenge to one's claim to know a **proposition,** one could only do one of three things. First, one could refuse to respond. But that, argued Agrippa, would be to accept that the **belief** is unsupported. Or, second, one could offer a further claim to know which supported the one already made. But since one can repeat the request for supporting grounds as regards this additional claim to know, one would then be obliged to offer a further claim to know in support of *this* claim. Accordingly, provided that one puts forward a new claim to know each time, this option will lead to an infinite regress. Or, finally, one could offer a further claim to know which supports the one already made but avoid the infinite regress by, at some point in the chain of grounds that ensues, putting forward a claim to know which has already appeared at a previous point in this chain. But that, claims Agrippa, is to argue in a circle. So the choice is between accepting that one's belief is ungrounded, offering an infinite chain of supporting grounds, or reasoning in a circle. Since none of these options is particularly appealing, it seems to follow that one is unable properly to enter a claim to know. **DHP**

See **circular reasoning; infinitism; Pyrrhonian scepticism; scepticism**

Further reading: Williams 2001, ch. 5

Alston, William Payne (1921–): An influential American philosopher who has contributed significantly to **epistemology,** philosophy of language, metaphysics, and philosophy of religion. In epistemology, Alston has made three main contributions. First, he has defended the position that there are no non-circular arguments for the reliability of sense-**perception.** Second, he has proposed that there is no such thing as *the* concept of **justification**. Rather, in his view the different theories of justification on the market show that there are many valuable epistemic features a belief might have. Finally, Alston has developed what he calls a 'doxastic practice approach' in which religious beliefs can have justification just in virtue of the experiences from which the beliefs arise. **MB**

See **perception; religious epistemology**

Further reading: Alston 1989, 1991, 1993a, 1993b, 2005

Analogy, argument from: A type of inductive argument, which proceeds by making use of certain analogies. Typically, an argument from analogy will have the following structure:

1. *R* is analogous to *S*.
2. *R* has property *a*.
3. So *S* has property *a* as well.

A famous argument from analogy is the one put forward by Paley in favour of the thesis that the universe is designed. Another famous argument from analogy is the argument in favour of the existence of **other minds. MB**

See **induction**

Further reading: Paley 1825

Analytic/synthetic: An important distinction in philosophy is the distinction between analytic and synthetic propositions. Examples of analytic propositions are:

1. All bodies are extended.
2. All bachelors are unmarried.

If one reads and understands these sentences, one cannot help but judge that they are true, just in virtue of the meaning of the words contained in them. In contrast, examples of synthetic propositions are:

3. All bodies are heavy.
4. Some bachelors are philosophers.

If one reads and understands these sentences, one cannot decide on the basis of the meaning of the words contained in them whether they are true or false. Whether (3) or (4) is true or false is to be determined by doing empirical research.

The distinction between analytic and synthetic propositions is especially important in the **epistemology** of **mathematical knowledge. MB**

See **mathematical knowledge**

Further reading: Kant 1998

Anti-realism: see **realism/anti-realism**

A priori/a posteriori: The notions *a priori* and *a posteriori* are epistemological notions and refer to how a **proposition** can be known. Broadly, propositions that can be known independently of any **experience** are *a priori* whereas propositions that cannot be known independently of any experience are *a posteriori*. Examples of *a priori* propositions are:

1. John knows that 1 + 1 equals 2.
2. John knows that every bachelor is unmarried.

Examples of *a posteriori* propositions are:

3. John knows that it is raining.
4. John knows that Jack is a bachelor.

An important topic in **epistemology** is whether *a priori* knowledge is possible, and if so, how. **MB**

See **analytic/synthetic; mathematical knowledge**

Further reading: BonJour 1998; Casullo 2003

Aquinas, Thomas (1227–74): An Italian theologian and philosopher, especially known for his *Summa Theologica*. Aquinas stands out as the primary spokesman of the school of natural theology. Central in the project of natural theology as developed by Aquinas is the distinction between two putative sources of religious **knowledge**. First, we can come to know religious propositions through the use of natural **reason**. However, we cannot know *all* religious propositions through the use of natural reason – some religious propositions exceed our limited cognitive capacities. Therefore, a second source of religious knowledge is needed which is divine **revelation**. Now the chief aim of natural theology is to try and acquire knowledge about God through offering arguments. Aquinas has offered five such arguments (the 'Five Ways'), the most famous of which might well be Aquinas's cosmological argument. Recently, arguments like these have been taken up by Swinburne and **Plantinga**. **MB**

See **religious epistemology; revelation**

Further reading: Swinburne 1979; Kretzmann and Stump 1993

Argument: An argument typically consists of one or more premises and a conclusion and its purpose is to present reasons to believe the conclusion. Arguments can be *valid*, meaning that if the premises were true, the conclusion would have to be true as well. Arguments can also be *sound*, meaning that (1) the argument is valid and (2) the premises and the conclusion are true. **MB**

See **analogy, argument from; deduction; induction**
Further reading: Fogelin and Sinnott-Armstrong 2001

Armstrong, D. M. (1926–): Australian philosopher whose main contribution in **epistemology** has been his defence of an influential version of **reliabilism**. Very roughly, this view identifies (non-inferential) **knowledge** with true **belief** that arises as a result of a law-like connection between the believer and the world – what has been referred to as the 'thermometer' theory of knowledge. **DHP**
See **reliabilism**
Further reading: Armstrong 1973

Assertion: Most commentators agree that asserting that *p* involves doing more than merely saying that *p*, although there is debate over just what else is required in this regard. In general, an assertion implies a certain confidence on the part of the agent in the **proposition** asserted, and also indicates a commitment to that proposition that will not easily be lost. Relatedly, an assertion often reflects the fact that the agent believes that she has met certain relevant **epistemic norms** as regards the proposition asserted. That is, to assert a proposition is typically to represent oneself as possessing good **evidence** in favour of it. Indeed, on one influential account of assertion – which has recently been defended by **Williamson** – to assert a propositon is to represent oneself as knowing that proposition. **DHP**
See **knowledge assertions**
Further reading: Williamson 1996b

Austin, J. L. (1911–60): Influential British philosopher who argued that philosophers should pay closer attention to the way the terms that are of interest to philosophers are employed in non-philosophical discourses. Austin's most important contribution to **epistemology** is probably the proto-**relevant alternatives** theory of **knowledge** that he advocated. Austin argued that one could only object to a claim to know by offering a concrete error-possibility that was contextually relevant. In particular, he argued that entering a challenge to a claim to know itself carries epistemic burdens such that a challenge of this sort cannot be coherently understood as being entirely baseless. One apparent consequence of this thesis is that sceptical challenges to our knowledge, which are typically not based on any specific grounds at all (on any specific *empirical* grounds at any rate), are ruled out as impermissible *tout court*. Austin's other contributions to epistemology include some subtle discussions of the way in which we use the phrase 'I know' (he argued that there were analogies in this respect to how we use the phrase 'I promise'), and of our everyday use of terms like 'looks', 'seems' and 'appears' in the traditional debates about **perception**. **DHP**

See **relevant alternatives**

Further reading: Austin 1961b, 1962a, 1962b; Warnock 1980

Avowals: Much of the philosophical interest in avowals derives from the treatment of this notion in the later work of **Wittgenstein**. Wittgenstein argues that we should treat at least some of our authoritative first-person claims about our psychological states – such as 'I am in pain' – not as descriptions of some 'inner' event that is based on an observation of an 'inner' realm, but rather as simply expressions or avowals. In doing so, argues Wittgenstein, we are able to rid ourselves of a misleading Cartesian picture of mind and world as consisting of two entirely separate realms (one that is 'inner' and one that is 'outer').

The idea is not to equate expressions of, say, pain, with the pain itself (as a behaviourist might be inclined to do), but rather to emphasise that, as he puts it, 'An "inner process" stands in need of outward criteria' (Wittgenstein 1953, S. 580). **DHP**

See **criteria; Wittgenstein, Ludwig**
Further reading: Wittgenstein 1953

Ayer, A. J. (1910–89): British philosopher, most noted for his defence of a radical form of **empiricism** known as **verificationism**. He argued that all meaningful statements are either **analytic** or **empirical**, in the sense of being verifiable by **experience**. In his **epistemology** he was an advocate of **phenomenalism**, arguing that we should understand material objects as logical constructions out of our (actual and possible) **sense-data**. He also put forward a verificationist response to the problem of **other minds**, arguing that the idea of empirically inaccessible (thought nonetheless *empirical*) truths about others' mental states was incoherent. Accordingly, he contended that we should treat such states as being essentially correlated with outward and empirically verifiable behaviour, and therefore defended a broadly behaviourist response to this problem. **DHP**

See **empiricism; other minds; phenomenalism; sense-data; verificationism**
Further reading: Ayer 1946, 1947, 1956; Foster 1985

Axiom: A **proposition** for which proof is not necessary. An axiom is often treated as basic in an epistemological sense (e.g. **self-evident**). Also, axioms have in the literature been treated as being necessary truths. **MB**

See **basic and non-basic belief; self-evident**
Further reading: Chisholm 1989

B

Basic and non-basic belief: Foundationalists argue that a subject's body of beliefs can be divided into two distinct categories. First, there are beliefs that are accepted on the evidential basis of other beliefs – this is the category of non-basic beliefs. Second, there are beliefs that are not accepted on the evidential basis of other beliefs – this is the category of basic beliefs. Thus, on the foundationalist picture, some beliefs are foundational whereas other beliefs are non-foundational and are accepted on the basis of the foundational beliefs. On this picture, the foundational beliefs form propositional **evidence** for the non-foundational beliefs. Typical examples of basic beliefs are **self-evident** beliefs (e.g. that $1 + 1$ equals 2) and beliefs about how one is appeared to (e.g. I am appeared to redly). The term 'basic belief' was coined by **Plantinga,** who adds that a belief is '*properly* basic' if the belief is justified, but not in virtue of being based on other justified beliefs. **MB**

    See **belief; coherentism; foundationalism; Plantinga, Alvin**

    Further reading: Plantinga 1983, 1993a, 1993b

Bayesian epistemology: A relatively new epistemological strand of thinking that is dependent on the ideas of Bayes (c. 1701–61). An essential element in Bayesian **epistemology** is the idea that there are degrees of **belief;** one can believe a particular **proposition** to a higher degree, or to a lower degree. And to what degree a subject believes a proposition is to be determined, on the Bayesian view, by using probability theory. Though Bayesian epistemology is very influential, some people object to the view as well, and one problem often cited is that the idea that we believe propositions with very specific degrees of strength seems counter-intuitive. **MB**

See **belief**

Further reading: Bovens and Hartmann 2004; Levy 1980

Begging the question: see **circular reasoning**

Belief: A crucial notion in **epistemology**, but one that has received surprisingly little attention when compared to other notions, is the notion of 'belief'. It is assumed by virtually all epistemologists that **knowledge** implies belief: one cannot know a **proposition** if one does not believe the proposition. One prominent exception in this respect is Radford, who argues that there are cases in which it is intuitively correct to say that the subject knows a proposition even if we also have the intuition that the subject does not believe the proposition in question.

Besides the question whether belief is a necessary condition for knowledge, epistemologists have also been interested in a couple of other questions. First, in the question of whether beliefs are real or not. With respect to this question, Fodor and Stalnaker defend doxastic realism (e.g. the claim that beliefs exist), while Dennett and Paul and Patricia Churchland defend doxastic anti-realism (e.g. the claim that beliefs do not exist). Second, in the question of whether one has responsibility for what one believes. With respect to this question, John Locke famously defends that there are indeed responsibilities attached to believing. Third, in the question of whether we can decide what to believe. This question is often answered in the negative: we have no voluntary control over what we believe. A fourth question in which epistemologists have been interested is how many relata the belief relation has. The usual answer is 'two': a subject and a proposition ('John believes that it rains'), but some (e.g. Swinburne) have defended a contrastive account of belief according to which the belief relation expresses a relation between a subject, a proposition and a set of contrastive propositions ('John believes that it rains rather than snows'). Finally, epistemologists have also been interested in the question of whether there are degrees of belief, with Bayesian epistemologists answering this question affirmatively. **MB**

See **Bayesian epistemology; contrastivism; deontologism, epistemic; doxastic voluntarism; knowledge**

Further reading: Helm 1994; Radford 1966; Swinburne 1983

Berkeley, George (1685–1753): Together with **Locke** and **Hume,** Berkeley belongs to the eighteenth-century British empiricists. Central in **empiricism** is the thought that there is only one way to know something to be real: through **experience.** Besides being an empiricist, Berkeley was also an idealist; he defended the position that everything that exists either is a mind or else is dependent on a mind. This position is captured in his famous dictum *esse est percipi* (to be is to be perceived) and is of great epistemological importance, particularly in discussions about **scepticism.** For if **idealism** is true, then we are only justified in believing in the appearance of an external world, and not in the existence of the external world itself. **MB**

See **empiricism; idealism; scepticism**

Further reading: Dancy 1987

Blame, epistemic: see **deontologism, epistemic**

BonJour, Laurence (1943–): One of the foremost epistemologists working in the United States today, BonJour is perhaps best known for his forceful defence of a version of **coherentism** and for his arguments against internalist versions of **foundationalism**. More recently, however, BonJour has changed his mind and now defends an internalist version of foundationalism. Elsewhere in **epistemology**, BonJour has put forward an important defence of *a priori* knowledge. **MB**

See **coherentism; foundationalism**

Further reading: BonJour 1985, 1998, 2002; BonJour and Sosa 2003

Brain in a vat: **Scepticism** about the external world is standardly triggered by the use of so-called **sceptical hypotheses**. One of the most famous of these sceptical hypotheses is the brain in a vat hypothesis, which was introduced by **Putnam**. According to this hypothesis, it might be the case that you are currently a brain floating in a vat filled with nutrient fluids. Your brain is furthermore attached to a powerful computer that provides you with all the experiences you currently have, including all the perceptual experiences.

It has been argued that taking this hypothesis seriously quickly leads to scepticism. Suppose, for instance, that you perceive your hands. The brain in a vat illusion of seeing your hands is subjectively indistinguishable from the real **perception** of your hands. From this, the sceptic concludes that we cannot know anything about the external world. The reason is that if we cannot know that the brain in a vat scenario is false, we cannot know ordinary propositions (such as that we have hands) as well, because the **truth** of those propositions implies that the brain in a vat scenario is false. Putnam has offered his own – content-externalist – line of response to this kind of sceptical reasoning, which makes use of semantic considerations. **MB**

See **Cartesian scepticism; content externalism/internalism; Putnam, Hilary; sceptical hypotheses; scepticism**
Further reading: Nuccetelli 2003; Putnam 1981, ch. 1; Wright 1991b

Cartesian scepticism: Historically, two of the most influential forms of **scepticism** have been the scepticism of the classical **Pyrrhonian** sceptics and the scepticism that **Descartes** considers (but doesn't accept) in his *Meditations*. As to the latter type of scepticism, its conclusion is that we know very little about the external world, and this of course conflicts with our intuitions in that respect. Descartes arrives at this conclusion by using so-called **sceptical hypotheses**: possibilities of error that are both incompatible with what we think to know and that cannot be subjectively distinguished from normal circumstances.

A famous example of a Cartesian sceptical hypothesis is the evil demon hypothesis according to which it might be the case that an evil demon ensures that you have all the perceptual experiences you currently have, although they are in fact false. Now, of course, it cannot be the case that you both have veridical perceptual experiences *and* are deceived by the evil demon; in effect, then, the evil demon hypothesis is incompatible with normal circumstances obtaining.

Since sceptical scenarios cannot be distinguished from normal circumstances, the Cartesian says that we cannot know that sceptical scenarios do not obtain, which in turn threatens the **certainty** of our ordinary beliefs. And, actually, this is exactly what Descartes wanted to achieve:

his sceptical project is part of his larger project of discovering the foundations of our body of knowledge, and an essential element in that project is the method of systematic **doubt**. Other types of Cartesian sceptical hypotheses that attempt to do more or less the same work as the evil demon hypothesis are the dream hypothesis and the **brain in a vat** hypothesis. **MB**

See **brain in a vat; certainty; Descartes, René; doubt; dreaming argument; sceptical hypotheses**

Further reading: Descartes 1975; Wright 1991a

Causal theory of knowledge: Causal theories of **knowledge** are primarily advanced to account for knowledge gained via **perception,** but have been put forward for other types of knowledge as well, such as knowledge gained via **memory.** In general, defenders of a causal theory hold that a true **belief** is an instance of knowledge just so long as the belief has the right sort of causal connection with the facts (they may also insist on further conditions obtaining as well, such as a **justification** or no-**defeater** condition). In the case of basic perceptual beliefs, for example, such as that the wall before me is red, the most natural causal connection would simply be that the belief was produced via a direct causal (perceptual) interaction with the red wall in question. Similar causal theories have also been proposed regarding justification. **DHP**

See **Goldman, Alvin; reliabilism**

Further reading: Goldman 1967

Certainty: Historically, much of the discussion of certainty has been bound up with the issue of **scepticism,** since it is commonly supposed that if certainty is a necessary condition for **knowledge** then the sceptic is on firm ground. (Indeed, the demand for certainty is an essential part of the sceptical project instigated by **Descartes.**) The reason why the demand for certainty is held to be a scepticism-friendly requirement on knowledge is that it is often thought that we are unable properly to regard ourselves as being certain about anything – or at least, anything **empirical** at any rate. Indeed, the demand for certainty is often equated with the demand for **infallibility**, such that one can only count oneself as properly certain about something provided one can be sure that there is no possibility that one is wrong. Since we are rarely, if ever, infallible in our beliefs, making certainty a requirement on knowledge would seem to undermine the possibility of our ever possessing widespread knowledge. In contrast to this picture, **Wittgenstein** argued that not only is certainty not a necessary condition for knowledge, but that we should not understand this notion in epistemic terms at all. Instead, our certain beliefs are those beliefs which perform what he calls a 'framework' role in our epistemic practices, in that they are the ungrounded backdrop against which we epistemically evaluate other propositions which we believe. **DHP**

See **absolute term; Descartes, René; doubt; infallibilism; infallibility; scepticism; Unger, Peter; Wittgenstein, Ludwig**

Further reading: Klein 1981; Unger 1975; Wittgenstein 1969

Charity, principle of: The principle of charity demands that in interpreting a speaker we must suppose that most of the speaker's beliefs are true. It is only on this supposition, argue its defenders – among them **Davidson** and **Quine** – that it would make sense to treat someone as speaking a language in the first place. If this principle is understood, as Davidson understands it, not just as a methodological principle but as a necessary characteristic of what it is to be a believer (so that one could only be a believer provided one has mostly true beliefs), then this principle would appear to have some dramatic implications for the problem of **scepticism** (it would also make Davidson committed to a version of **content externalism**). Davidson has tried to draw out some of these anti-sceptical implications with the use of his **omniscient interpreter** thought-experiment. **DHP**

See **content externalism/internalism; Davidson, Donald; omniscient interpreter; scepticism**

Further reading: Davidson 1986

Chicken sexer: Along with the 'clairvoyant' example, the chicken sexer example is one of the most famous cited in the debate regarding the **externalism/internalism** distinction. The example concerns an agent who, by being raised around chickens, acquires a highly reliable ability to distinguish between male and female chicks. Crucially, however, this agent has false beliefs about how she is discriminating these chicks, believing that it is due to something distinctive that she is seeing or touching (it's actually due to her attuned sense of smell). Some formulations of the example also add that the agent lacks a good reason for thinking that she is reliable in this respect (she hasn't verified her success ratio, for example). Either way, it seems implausible to suppose that this agent has a **justification** – in any normal sense of the term at least – for what she believes regarding the sex of these chicks. Nevertheless, on certain externalist views of **knowledge**, such as **reliabilism**, the agent will count as having knowledge in this case. The example is thus meant to help us to refine our intuitions regarding these sorts of theories of knowledge. **DHP**

See **externalism/internalism; reliabilism; virtue epistemology**

Further reading: Zagzebski 1996, pt III, ss. 2.1. and 4.1

Chisholm, Roderick (1916–99): American philosopher who has had an extremely large impact on all areas of philosophy, including **epistemology**. His best-known contributions to epistemology are his defence of **internalism** about justification and his defence of a particularist approach to the analysis of **knowledge**. As to the first point, Chisholm defends that we can know whether our beliefs are justified *from the inside out*, just by sitting in our armchairs. As to the second point, Chisholm defends that we can have knowledge of some truths about the external world prior to our knowing what the method for acquiring that knowledge is. **MB**

See **externalism/internalism; justification; criterion, problem of the**

Further reading: Chisholm 1957, 1973, 1989; Kornblith 2003; Sosa 2003

Circular reasoning: An **argument** is circular when one of the premises in the argument presupposes the **truth** of the conclusion: in accepting the premise of the argument, one has already implicitly accepted the conclusion. Circular reasoning is also knows as *petitio principii* and begging the question. One famous argument that is often thought to beg the question, is **Moore**'s argument in favour of **knowledge** of the external world. Also, **Alston** has famously showed that every attempt to establish the reliability of sense-**perception** is doomed to be circular. This is because in arguing for the reliability of sense-perception one will always be making use of that very source. **MB**

See **Moorean responses to scepticism**

Further reading: Alston 1993b

Clairvoyance: Cases in which clairvoyance figures have been introduced in the epistemological literature by Laurence **BonJour,** and are particularly important in the **externalism/internalism** debate. BonJour uses these cases in order to argue against externalist theories of **knowledge.** The clairvoyance case (or at least one version of it) concerns a perfectly reliable clairvoyant – who is called Norman – who possesses no evidence for or against the thesis that he is a perfectly reliable clairvoyant. At one point, Norman comes to believe that the President is in New York on the basis of his clairvoyant powers. He has no evidence for or against this **belief.** Yet the belief is true: the President is in New York (see BonJour 1985: 41). Now in this particular case, BonJour argues, we will have the intuition that Norman is irrational in accepting this belief. Externalists will have to say, however, that Norman is justified in believing that the President is in New York, and that he furthermore knows this – which gives a counter-intuitive result. So the moral of the case is that internalist justification is necessary for knowledge. **MB**

See **BonJour, Laurence; chicken sexer; externalism/ internalism; reliabilism**

Further reading: BonJour 1985; BonJour and Sosa 2003

Closure, principle of: The closure principle is a principle that is found highly intuitive by most epistemologists, and roughly expresses the idea that **deduction** transmits **knowledge.** It has proven surprisingly hard to present a formalised version of the closure principle. On most standard formalisations, the principle states that if a person knows a **proposition,** and if that person knows that that proposition implies another proposition, then the person knows the other proposition as well. For instance, if John knows that it rains, and if John knows that if it rains, then it does not snow, then John knows that it does not snow. Recently, the closure principle has undergone a lot of refinements. **Williamson**, for instance, adds that one has to *competently deduce* the second proposition from the first (thereby coming to believe the second proposition) in order to know the second proposition. The closure principle figures essentially in the debate surrounding radical **scepticism**. Philosophers like **Dretske** and **Nozick** are famous for having denied closure in order to save our everyday knowledge. Without closure in play, they argue, we can know that we have hands, and we can know that if we have hands, then we are no brains in vats, *without* having to know that we are no brains in vats. **MB**

See **brain in a vat; Dretske, Fred; Nozick, Robert; relevant alternatives; scepticism; tracking**

Further reading: Dretske 1970; Nozick 1981; Williamson 2000

Coady, C. A. J. (1936–): Influential Australian philosopher most noted in **epistemology** for his contribution to the epistemology of **testimony**. Coady argues against what he claims is a Humean thesis as regards testimony which seeks to reduce the epistemic status of our testimony-based beliefs to non-testimonial sources. In its place, he offers a broadly Reidean theory of the epistemology of testimony which accords testimony-based beliefs a default epistemic status. It is only by allowing such a default status to our testimony-based beliefs, argues Coady, that we could acquire a language and thereby understand testimonial assertions in the first place. **DHP**

See **credulity, principle of; Hume, David; Reid, Thomas; testimony**

Further reading: Coady 1992

***Cogito*, the:** In his *Meditations*, **Descartes** famously tried to discover the certain foundations of our **knowledge**. The starting-point of this quest for **certainty** is systematic **doubt**: by doubting the basic principles on which all our beliefs rest, Descartes hopes to find the Archimedean point that will be the basis for the **belief** system that will be built upon it. This first point of certainty is the existence of the self. What remains after the introduction of systematic doubt is the conviction that one can still think. But if one thinks, one surely must exist: 'Cogito, ergo sum'('I am thinking, therefore I exist'). **MB**

See **Cartesian scepticism; certainty; dreaming argument; infallibilism; sceptical hypotheses**

Further reading: Cottingham 1992; Descartes 1975

Cognition: Broadly speaking, cognition and **knowledge** are co-referential, in that to say that someone has cognised something is usually thereby to say that she knows it, and vice versa. More strictly, however, one can regard cognition as a broader category than knowledge, at least when it comes to **propositional knowledge** at any rate. For example, often the term 'cognition' is used in such a way that it allows types of knowledge which are not obviously propositional in form, such as **ability knowledge** or **knowledge by acquaintance**. Moreover, the term cognition also covers what is known as 'sub-personal' epistemic states which are not clearly cases of knowledge at all (of *any* type). For instance, it has been noted by psychologists that we have cognitive traits which enable us reliably to gain true beliefs where the functioning of these traits has nothing to do with our conscious thoughts or goals. On a broad reading of the term, one might refer to the states that result as 'knowledge', but even if that term is not applicable here, the term 'cognition' certainly is. **DHP**

See **cognitive faculties; reliabilism; virtue epistemology**

Further reading: Goldman 1986

Cognitive faculties: One's cognitive faculties are typically taken to be one's naturally occurring **belief**-forming traits, such as one's perceptual belief-forming traits that are connected up with one's senses, and perhaps also other belief-forming traits such as those involved in **introspection**. Equally, however, one might extend the term so that it also covers acquired belief-forming traits, such as, for example, the kind of observational skills that one might acquire in virtue of being an avid bird-watcher. Typically, talk of cognitive faculties is meant to draw a contrast with belief-forming traits that involve a substantial degree of reflection on the part of the agent. One can, for example, appropriately form one's basic perceptual beliefs spontaneously without needing to reflect at all on the belief-forming activity in question. Compare such basic perceptual cases with the belief-forming skills employed by the judge presiding over a murder trial. Here spontaneity seems inappropriate, and the need for reflection on the considerations in play paramount. Indeed, some have argued that there is a 'sub-personal' element to the belief-forming processes involved in our most basic cognitive faculties, in the sense that the agent concerned cannot really be held responsible for the beliefs gained. Relatedly, it has been suggested that genuine **knowledge** can never consist of merely true belief gained solely via a reliable cognitive faculty – as some versions of **reliabilism** maintain – but rather also demands the exercise of an **intellectual virtue**, where the latter essentially involves some kind of reflective component. **DHP**

See **cognition; faculty reliabilism; intellectual virtues; reliabilism; virtue epistemology**

Further reading: Goldman 1986; Sosa 1991; Zagzebski 1996

Cohen, Stewart (1952–): American philosopher whose principal contribution to **epistemology** has been a form of attributer **contextualism**. Along with other contemporary figures, such as **DeRose** and **Lewis**, Cohen argues that 'knows' is a context-sensitive term where the relevant context is that of the one who ascribes **knowledge**. Accordingly, whether or not an **assertion** of the sentence '*S* knows that *p*' expresses a truth will depend on the contextual standards in operation in the ascriber's context. If they are low, then such an assertion will tend to express a truth, while if they are high, then such an assertion will tend to express a falsehood. Cohen argues that this sort of thesis can help us to deal with a number of the key problems in epistemology, including the problem of **scepticism** and the **lottery paradox**. DHP

See **contextualism; lottery paradox; scepticism**

Further reading: Cohen 2000

Coherentism: The central metaphor used to illustrate **foundationalism** is that of the pyramid: our body of **knowledge** is like a pyramid in that a set of foundational beliefs transfers justification on all the beliefs that rest on the foundational beliefs. In contrast, the central metaphor used to illustrate coherentism is that of the raft: our body of knowledge is like a raft in that it is not anchored by anything. What justifies a particular **belief** according to the coherentist is just that it coheres with the rest of one's belief system. An important question is, of course, what 'coherence' is. It does not only mean that a particular belief is consistent with one's other beliefs, it can also mean something stronger, namely that a particular belief is supported by one's other beliefs.

An influential objection to coherentism – due to **Plantinga** – might further clarify the coherentist position. Imagine Ric who is climbing Guide's Wall. Enjoying the view, he forms the beliefs that Cascade Canyon is down to his left, that the cliffs of Mount Owen are directly in front of him, and that there is a hawk gliding in lazy circles 200 feet below him. But suddenly Ric is struck by a burst of high-energy cosmic radiation, which results in his beliefs being fixed: they no longer respond to changes in his environment. That night at the opera house, Ric continues to believe that Cascade Canyon is down to his left, that the cliffs of Mount Owen are directly in front of him, and that there is a hawk gliding in lazy circles 200 feet below him (Plantinga 1993: 179). The crucial thing to see here is that *his beliefs are coherent* and must, according to the coherentist, therefore be justified. But saying that his beliefs are coherent is intuitively incorrect. **MB**

See **basic and non-basic belief; foundationalism; foundherentism; justification; Plantinga, Alvin**

Further reading: BonJour 1985; Plantinga 1993a, 1993b; Sosa 1980

Common sense: A position in **epistemology** (and philosophy in general) according to which every epistemological position that aims to be adequate should conform to the intuitions ordinary people have about epistemological issues. This methodological starting-point enables the common sense philosopher to respond in a very particular way to the problem of radical **scepticism**. Common sense philosophers respond to this problem by claiming – *contra* the sceptic – that we do know a lot of the things about the external world we ordinarily think to know, and, by consequence, that we do know the denials of sceptical hypotheses as well. An important objection to this common sense argument against scepticism is that it begs the question. Common sense philosophers who are particularly noteworthy for their contributions to epistemology are **Reid, Moore** and **Chisholm. MB**

See **Chisholm, Roderick; Moore, G. E.; scepticism; Reid, Thomas**

Further reading: Greco 2000; Van Woudenberg 2004

Content externalism/internalism: Content externalists hold that the content of at least some of an agent's mental states can be determined by environmental factors – that is 'external' factors which are outside the skin of the agent. Content internalists, in contrast, reject this claim, maintaining instead that the content of an agent's mental states can only be affected by what is within the skin of the agent. The motivation for the content externalist view comes from a number of sources.

To begin with, there are the famous thought-experiments offered by **Putnam** and others which appear to support a causal theory of reference which entails content externalism. Perhaps the most famous of these examples – and one which has direct epistemological ramifications – is Putnam's **brain in a vat** example. According to Putnam, in order to have thoughts about brains one must either have had the appropriate casual contact with brains or be part of a language community some of the members of which have had the appropriate casual contact with brains. Crucially, however, one who has always been a brain in a vat and who has never had any causal contact with other language users could never have been in the appropriate causal contact with brains. Accordingly, in such a case one would not be able to think the thought that one is, or is not, a brain in a vat (one would think a different thought instead, one that had a different content). Putnam and others have taken this line of argument to show that any form of **scepticism** which trades on the assumption that even if one had always been a brain in a vat one could still think the same thoughts as one who had never been a brain in a vat must be false.

A slightly different motivation for content externalism, but one which has also been held to have anti-sceptical ramifications, is the defence of the **principle of charity** offered by such figures as **Davidson** and **Quine**. This principle holds that one can only interpret another speaker on the supposition that most of that speaker's beliefs are true. Crucially, however, Davidson treats this principle as being more than merely a methodological constraint on interpretation, arguing that it follows from this principle that '**belief** is in its nature veridical' (1986: 314). If this is right, then this too would be a form of content externalism, in that the very fact that one has mental states of a certain sort (in this case beliefs) would entail that many of one's beliefs are true and this, in turn, would have ramifications for how the world is. Moreover, this would have implications for any sceptical argument which presupposes that it is possible to have beliefs which are mostly false. Davidson draws out some of these anti-sceptical implications of the principle of charity by using his **omniscient interpreter** example.

A third form of content externalism which has important epistemological implications is the view proposed by **McDowell**. According to McDowell, the content of one's **experience** can be dependent upon facts about the world. In particular, McDowell rejects what is known as the **highest common factor** view as regards perceptual experience. This view holds that since one's perceptual experiences may well not correspond with the world in the manner that one supposes (as happens when one is deceived), it follows that the content of one's experiences must be understood in phenomenal terms (that is, so that the content of one's experience is always concerned with how the world appears and not how it is). In contrast, McDowell maintains that just so long as one is undeceived in one's perceptual experiences, then those experiences can be of the world directly, such that one directly experiences how the world is. Since one's perceptual experiences are (intuitively at any rate) part of one's mental states, it follows that McDowell is committed to a form of content externalism which holds that the content of some of one's mental states is in part determined by environmental factors. Like Putnam and Davidson, McDowell also draws anti-sceptical implications from this thesis, arguing that versions of scepticism which presuppose that the content of one's experiences must always be understood in phenomenal terms are erroneous.

Aside from the anti-sceptical implications of content externalism, there are also two further issues related to this thesis that have been widely discussed by epistemologists. The first concerns the consistency of our **first-person authority** regarding our **knowledge** of our mental states with the content externalist thesis. Since we seem to know what the content of our mental states are in an *a priori* fashion via **introspection,** and since we also appear to know the truth of content externalism *a priori*, through philosophical analysis, it appears to follow that when it comes to the relevant mental states we can know truths about the world via an *a priori* means, which is counter-intuitive. The second main topic of interest to epistemologists in this respect concerns what ramifications, if any, content externalism has for the **externalism/internalism** distinction in **epistemology. DHP**

See **brain in a vat; charity, principle of; Davidson, Donald; first-person authority; highest common factor;**

Putnam, Hilary; McDowell, John; omniscient interpreter; reasons; scepticism

Further reading: Davidson 1986; McDowell 1994; Nuccetelli 2003; Putnam 1981, ch. 1

Contextualism: Contextualist theories of **knowledge** have primarily been introduced in the literature with the aim of explaining some puzzling cases in which the interests and purposes of the attributers of knowledge seem to determine whether a particular subject knows or not. Contextualist theories have also been put forward in order to provide a solution to the sceptical paradox.

One of the most hotly debated positions in contemporary **epistemology**, contextualist theories come in many forms. These forms can be divided into two main brands of contextualism: first, a brand of contextualism that makes the context of the attributer of knowledge crucial; second, a brand of contextualism that makes the context of the subject of knowledge crucial. Defenders of attributer contextualism are **DeRose, Cohen** and **Lewis,** whereas defenders of subject contextualism are Annis, **Williams,** and Hawthorne.

The best-known type of attributer contextualism probably is the one that can be labelled 'semantic contextualism' and that is advocated by such figures as DeRose and Cohen. According to semantic contextualism as defended by DeRose, 'knows' is an indexical (just like words as 'I' and 'here' are) and it is this feature that ensures the context-dependent truth-value of knowledge sentences. And according to semantic contextualism as defended by Cohen, the truth-conditions of knowledge sentences vary in accordance with features of the conversational context of the attributer of knowledge, because knowledge implies '**justification**' and justification comes in degrees.

Another type of attributer contextualism can be labelled 'relevant alternatives contextualism'. According to this type of contextualism, initiated by **Austin** and **Dretske** and advocated by Lewis, knowledge requires the elimination of a particular set of relevant alternatives – and whether an alternative is relevant depends on features of the conversational context.

The best-known types of subject contextualism probably are the ones defended by Williams and Hawthorne. Williams argues in a broadly Wittgensteinean fashion for the thesis that in different contexts different inferential structures are in play that govern what may be inferred relative to what. And Hawthorne argues for a position which he calls 'sensitive moderate invariantism' on which the attention and interests of a subject partly determine whether the subject has knowledge. **MB**

See **assertion; contrastivism; knowledge assertions; relevant alternatives; scepticism**

Further reading: Cohen 2000; DeRose 1995; Hawthorne 2004; Lewis 1996; Sosa 1986

Contingent/necessary: The contingent/necessary distinction is an important distinction in metaphysics. A **proposition** is contingently true if it could have been false (or in the language of possible worlds: it is true in the actual world, but not true in every possible world). It is true, for instance, that I am currently working at my computer, but this might not have been the case. Propositions are necessarily true, by contrast, if they cannot possibly be false (or in the language of possible worlds: they are true in the actual world and in every possible world). Propositions such as '$1 + 1 = 2$', or 'All bachelors are unmarried' are usually regarded as being necessary. **MB**

See *a priori/a posteriori*; **analytic/synthetic**

Further reading: Plantinga 1974

Contrastivism: One plausible way of thinking about **knowledge** is that 'knows' expresses a relation. The usual assumption is that this relation is a two-place relation between a subject and a **proposition** ('John knows that it rains'). Contrastivists challenge this assumption and defend that the knowledge relation is a three-place relation between a subject, a proposition and a set of contrastive propositions. Knowing a proposition is always knowing that proposition against the background of one or more contrastive propositions. Knowledge attributions of the form 'S knows that p' are thus treated as elliptical: they need to be completed with the set of contrastive propositions Q.

The contrastivist view has emerged only recently and is related to both **contextualism** and **relevant alternatives** theory. What contrastivism shares with contextualism is that the context of the attributer of knowledge determines what the contrastive propositions are with respect to which a subject knows a **proposition**. What contrastivism shares with relevant alternatives theory is that in order to know, one must be able to eliminate various relevant alternatives (or contrastive propositions). Contrastivists claim that their theory can solve the sceptical paradox – and that it does so without claiming that 'knows' is an indexical (as contextualists do), and without denying the **closure principle** for knowledge (as relevant alternatives theorists do). **MB**

See **closure, principle of; contextualism; relevant alternatives; scepticism**

Further reading: Blaauw 2004; Schaffer 2004, 2005a; Stalnaker 2004

Counterexamples: Most of the central questions in **epistemology** are conceptual questions, such as 'What is **knowledge?**', or 'What is **justification?**'. Often, epistemologists try to answer these questions by using the method of conceptual analysis. Broadly, this method boils down to trying to state the individually necessary and jointly sufficient conditions that must be satisfied for the concept in question to obtain. In effect, conceptual analysis often, if not always, proceeds by way of providing counterexamples to existing conceptual analyses. These counterexamples show that an existing analysis of a particular concept is incorrect, either because one of the conditions is not necessary for the concept in question to obtain, or because the set of conditions is not sufficient for the concept in question to obtain. The most famous type of counterexample may well be the so-called **Gettier cases** which were put forward in order to show that the **tripartite definition of knowledge** in terms of justified true **belief** was incorrect. **MB**

See **Gettier cases**

Further reading: Jackson 1998, ch. 2; Weatherson 2003

Credulity, principle of: According to **Reid**, it is an innate feature of human nature that we are disposed unreflectively to give credence to what others tell us. He offers a pragmatic defence of such a disposition, arguing that if we were instead disposed to meet testimonial assertions with **scepticism** (such that we were always inclined to seek additional independent grounds in favour of what is being asserted), then this would prove a severe handicap to the acquisition of **knowledge**. Reid also advocates a related principle, what he calls a 'principle of veracity', which states that we are similarly disposed to speak the **truth** in our assertions. **DHP**

See **Reid, Thomas; testimony**

Further reading: Coady 1992

Criteria: Interest in criteria by epistemologists has tended to focus on the treatment of this notion put forward by **Wittgenstein**, especially regarding his remarks on the criterial relationship between pain and pain behaviour. The problem posed by this relationship is that it seems problematic to say, as a behaviourist might be inclined to claim, that pain *just is* pain behaviour, since, amongst other things, such a view would appear to obliterate the 'internal' dimension to pain altogether. Equally, however, supposing pain to be an entirely 'inner' event that is in principle divorceable from the pain behaviour itself would also be problematic. One reason why such a view would be objectionable is that it would appear to make it merely a contingent fact that pain is associated with pain behaviour. By claiming that there is a criterial relationship between pain and pain behaviour, Wittgenstein is rejecting both of these positions and offering instead a view that lies between them. The idea is that there is an *a priori evidential* connection between pain and pain behaviour, in the sense that it is an *a priori* matter that pain behaviour is **evidence** for pain (this evidential connection is not, for example, something that we discover through observation). The advantage to this view of pain is that it is able to show that there is an *a priori* connection between pain and pain behaviour, and thus between the 'inner' and the 'outer' aspects of pain phenomena, without thereby equating the former to the latter. It has been argued that such a criterial account could also have application elsewhere in philosophy. **DHP**

See **Wittgenstein, Ludwig**

Further reading: Wittgenstein 1953

Criterion, problem of the: A problem coined by **Chisholm**. In order to know whether things really are as they appear to be, Chisholm says, we need some kind of method that will help us distinguish appearances from reality. However, in order to know that the method delivers the correct results, we have to know whether it is successful in distinguishing appearances from reality. But in order to know *that*, we already must be able to distinguish appearances from reality. We are thus caught in a circle. Chisholm proposes three ways out of the circle. First, we can be methodists: we can know what the method to attain **knowledge** is before we have any knowledge. Second, we can be sceptics: because we are caught in the circle, we cannot know anything. Third, we can be particularists: we can have knowledge before we even know what the method to attain knowledge is. Chisholm's favoured approach is particularism, which is clearly a **common sense** position. MB

See **Chisholm, Roderick; common sense; scepticism**
Further reading: Chisholm 1973; Kornblith 2003

Davidson, Donald (1930–2003): An American philosopher, Davidson's influence on contemporary **epistemology** – and, indeed, on contemporary philosophy in general – has been immense. The key contribution made by Davidson to epistemological debate arises out of his advocacy of the **principle of charity**, a principle that he inherited from **Quine**. Although this is primarily just a methodological constraint on interpretation which demands that one should treat a speaker as having mostly true beliefs, Davidson understands this principle in far more robust terms as highlighting how it is constitutive of the notion of an agent *qua* believer that most of the beliefs of that agent are true. Davidson is thus led to a form of **content externalism** which holds that the mere fact that one has mental states of a certain sort imposes limitations on how the world could be. One interesting consequence of this content externalist element to his view is that whilst Davidson's epistemological position is broadly coherentist, by allying **coherentism** to content externalism Davidson is able to claim that there is an essential connection between coherence and **truth** (such that a coherent set of beliefs will be, for the most part, a true one). Davidson is therefore apparently able to resolve one of the key problems facing coherentism, which is that it seems unable to account for this truth-connection. Using his **omniscient interpreter** thought-experiment, Davidson also draws an anti-sceptical moral from his epistemology by arguing that any form of **scepticism** which presupposes that one could have mostly false beliefs must be false.

Davidson has also made a distinctive contribution to the theory of truth, arguing that truth cannot be defined and should therefore be treated as an indefinable primitive. **DHP**

See **charity, principle of; coherentism; content externalism/internalism; omniscient interpreter; scepticism**

Further reading: Davidson 1986, 2001a, 2001b, 2004; LePore 1986

Deduction: Type of inference where the conclusion is entailed by the premises. Deductive inferences are the opposite of inductive inferences, where the conclusion is not entailed by the premises. **MB**

See **abductive reasoning; argument; induction**

Further reading: Fogelin and Sinnott-Armstrong 2001

Deductive-nomological model: see **explanation**

Defeasibility: The epistemic support one has for a **belief** is defeasible when it could be undermined (or at least weakened) by further **evidence**. For example, while I might well have excellent evidence for believing that the defendant is guilty, that evidence could be defeated if further evidence came to light, such as evidence which indicated that one of the main trial witnesses was lying. In general, there are two ways in which the defeasible epistemic support one has for a belief can be defeated. The first is when one acquires evidence which calls into question the epistemic pedigree of the evidential basis of one's belief. This is usually known as 'undercutting' evidence, and this is the kind of defeating evidence that is in play in the trial case that was just considered. A different kind of defeating evidence is evidence that independently indicates that the proposition believed is false – what is usually known as 'overriding' evidence. In terms of our trial example, an instance of this might be where one discovers a DNA sample which, while not directly conflicting with any of the other evidence cited at the trial, nevertheless indicates that the defendant could not be guilty of the crime in question. When further evidence comes to light which undermines the epistemic status of one's belief, the new evidence is called a **defeater**. DHP

See **defeater; evidence**

Further reading: Pollock 1986

Defeater: Suppose that you believe that your flatmate has started smoking again on the basis of smelling a cigarette odour in the living room. Later on, you bump into your flatmate, point out that you smelled cigarette odour earlier that day, and accuse him of having started smoking again. But your flatmate responds: 'No, I haven't started smoking again. I just had John over for dinner last night, and he is a terrible chain-smoker.' Most probably, you will now no longer believe that your flatmate has started smoking again; you have acquired a *defeater* for this be-lief. So if a particular belief gets undermined by further evidence, this further evidence is a defeater for the epis-temic status of that belief. **MB**

See **defeasibility; evidence**

Further reading: Bergmann 1997; Pollock 1974, 1986

Deflationism, epistemic: In the theory of **truth**, deflationism is the view that truth is not nearly as philosophically impor-tant as many have supposed, and this proposal is often supplemented with the contention that there is nothing substantial that connects all instances of truth together. Similar claims are made by epistemic deflationists, the most famous of which is probably **Williams**. Williams argues that the mistake made by traditional epistemol-ogists, and which leads to the problem of **scepticism**, is to take for granted what he calls 'epistemological real-ism'. This is realism about the objects of epistemological enquiry, and essentially manifests itself in the claim that there is an innate structure to all instances of **knowledge** which reveals itself under philosophical reflection when one abstracts away from contextual considerations. In contrast, Williams contends that the epistemic role that a **proposition** plays depends upon the context in which the **belief** in that proposition appears. Williams thus ad-vances a radical form of **contextualism** which treats the structure of knowledge as an essentially context-bound matter. A similar – though less worked-out – deflationary account of knowledge can also be found in the work of **Rorty.**

A different form of epistemic deflationism can be found in **naturalised epistemology** and in the work of such thinkers as Sartwell and **Foley**. Naturalised epistemologists tend to deflate the epistemological project by regarding it as a largely **empirical** affair, one that is best conducted by cognitive scientists than in an *a priori* fashion by philosophers. In contrast, Sartwell and Foley retain the *a priori* dimension to their exploration of knowledge, but nevertheless end up deflating the notion by claiming that we can dispense with an epistemic condition – that is, a condition, defined in terms other than true belief, that turns true belief into knowledge. In Sartwell, this thesis consists of the radical claim that knowledge is nothing other than true belief. Foley's position, in contrast, is much more modest, but no less controversial. He claims that knowledge is nothing more than true belief plus a further contextually-determined set of true beliefs. DHP

See **contextualism; naturalised epistemology; scepticism**

Further reading: Foley (forthcoming); Pritchard 2004; Quine 1969a; Sartwell 1991; Williams 1991

Deontologism, epistemic: Influential view in **epistemology** that has been defended by such figures as **Locke, Descartes, BonJour, Chisholm,** and Ginet. According to epistemic deontologism, a subject's **belief** in a **proposition** is an instance of **knowledge** if and only if the subject doesn't violate any epistemic duties in believing that proposition. Different philosophers have proposed different epistemic duties in this respect. For instance, according to (one interpretation of) Locke, among our epistemic duties are (1) to put our faith in things only upon good **reason,** and (2) to seek the **truth**. According to Clifford, we have a duty always to follow our **evidence** – thus paving the way for his famous dictum: 'It is wrong always, everywhere, and for anyone, to believe anything upon insufficient evidence.' According to **James**, we have a duty to know the truth and to avoid error. And according to Chisholm, finally, we have a duty to try our best to ensure that for every proposition that we consider, we only accept the proposition if it is true.

Epistemic deontologism is subject to one severe type of criticism – put forward by Alston – that many find compelling. According to this criticism, epistemic deontologism presupposes that we can control what we believe: the notion 'duty to do something' is only appropriate if one can choose not to do that something. So if we claim that there are duties regarding doxastic attitudes such as 'believing', it follows that we have some amount of voluntary control over what we believe. But this is not the case. Hence, Alston argues, epistemic deontologism fails to be a convincing theory because it has this implausible consequence. **MB**

See **doxastic voluntarism; evidentialism; norms, epistemic**

Further reading: Alston 1989

DeRose, Keith (1963–): One of the foremost figures in contemporary **epistemology**, DeRose's main contribution to epistemology is his defence of epistemological **contextualism**. DeRose's idea is that we should respond to the problem of **scepticism** by maintaining that, though it might be true in some sceptical contexts that we don't know that we have hands, this is certainly not true in *all* contexts. In particular, in contexts in which the standards for knowledge are low, we can both know that we have hands and that **sceptical hypotheses** are false. DeRose is influenced by common sense philosophers such as **Reid** and **Moore**. **MB**

See **contextualism; modal epistemology; scepticism**

Further reading: DeRose 1995, 2002

Descartes, René (1596–1650): One of the founding figures of modern **epistemology**, Descartes is especially renowned for his attempt to find the indubitable ground on which all our **knowledge** rests. His method of 'systematic **doubt**' led him to consider such **sceptical hypotheses** as that one might currently be dreaming or that one is currently deceived by an evil demon. The building anew of the belief system is initiated by the famous '*Cogito, ergo sum*' ('I think, therefore I am'), which is the one thing that is beyond all **doubt**. Descartes's most famous work is his *Meditations on First Philosophy*, which was first published in 1641. MB

See **Cartesian scepticism;** *Cogito,* **the; doubt; dreaming argument**

Further reading: Cottingham 1992; Descartes 1975

Dewey, John (1859–1952): American philosopher and one of the key exponents of **pragmatism**. He emphasised a dynamic understanding of **knowledge** which focused on enquiry and accused much of epistemological theorising as being predicated on a 'spectator' view of knowledge that detaches knowledge from enquiry and which therefore treats the relationship between the knower and the fact known as an entirely passive one. DHP

See **pragmatism**

Further reading: Campbell 1995; Dewey 1969–90

Direct/indirect knowledge: On the standard view, we have direct (or immediate) **knowledge** of a **proposition** if our knowledge of this proposition isn't based on our knowledge of other propositions. Accordingly, we have indirect (or mediate) knowledge of a proposition if our knowledge *is* based on our knowledge of other propositions. It is usually thought that we have immediate knowledge of our own mental states: if I am in pain, for instance, I know this in a direct way – I don't infer 'that I have pain' from another proposition (for example, 'My finger is broken'). **Memory** is also thought to provide us with immediate knowledge. And some epistemologists (**Plantinga,** for instance) argue that we can have immediate knowledge of religious propositions. **MB**

See **foundationalism; knowledge by acquaintance/ knowledge by description; self-evident**

Further reading: Alston 1983

Dogmatism: Dogmatism is a position that is important in the context of discussions about radical **scepticism.** It can be applied to both perceptual **justification** and perceptual **knowledge.** The dogmatist about justification will argue that we can be justified in believing certain propositions even if we are unable to provide any **argument** in favour of the **belief** in question. Here the idea is that if one has a certain perceptual **experience** in which a certain state of affairs seems to be the case, this alone is enough to bestow a certain amount of justification on one's corresponding belief. The dogmatist about knowledge will add that the justification some beliefs have in this dogmatist fashion will be enough to ensure that the belief is also an instance of knowledge. **MB**

See **justification; perception; scepticism**

Further reading: Pryor 2000

Doubt: 'Doubting a **proposition**' is an attitude towards a proposition that is characterised by a lack of **certainty** in the target proposition. Though doubt is a propositional attitude, we can also use the word 'doubt' in a weaker sense to mean that one cannot decide whether a proposition or its denial is the case, as in 'John is in doubt about whether Paris is capital of France or of Belgium'.

The notion of doubt is of crucial importance in **epistemology**. For instance, **Descartes**'s general methodological strategy in epistemology was that of doubting all that is not certain so that he could discover the secure epistemic foundations. Though the usual idea is that every proposition is logically open to doubt, some philosophers have put forward propositions that cannot coherently be doubted. Descartes, again, holds that we cannot doubt that we exist. And **Wittgenstein** defends that there are 'hinge propositions' that cannot be coherently doubted. Discussions about doubt figure especially in debates about radical **scepticism**, where **sceptical hypotheses** are introduced in order to cast doubt on whether we do indeed know the things we ordinarily think to know. **MB**

See **certainty; hinge propositions; indubitability**

Further reading: Wittgenstein 1969

Doxastic voluntarism: To what extent do we have control over our beliefs? If one thinks that one has control over what one believes, even if only indirectly, then one is a doxastic voluntarist. The importance of this issue for **epistemology** rests in how it is often thought that to be justified in holding a **belief** one must conform to one's epistemic duties. If one has no control over one's beliefs, however, then, given the further principle that 'ought implies can' at any rate, it seems to follow that one cannot be held to account for forming beliefs which do not conform with one's epistemic duties.

It is certainly true that a lot of our most basic sensory beliefs are spontaneous, and so formed involuntarily. Nevertheless, this need not settle the issue of doxastic voluntarism, since it could be that one has a substantial degree of control over one's other beliefs, such as one's theoretical beliefs, and that control in this area of one's

beliefs can have an indirect effect on what one spontaneously believes in the sensory case. Alternatively, one
might deny the 'ought implies can' principle, at least as it
applies here, thereby severing the need for doxastic voluntarism to be true in order for justification to demand
the satisfaction of one's epistemic duties. **DHP**

See **deontologism, epistemic**

Further reading: Feldman 1988; Heil 1983

Dreaming argument: The dreaming argument is a familiar
sceptical argument, with the particular variant of this argument that is of most interest to contemporary epistemologists due to **Descartes**. Descartes notes that while he
believes that he is sitting in his armchair beside the fire,
it is entirely possible that he may be at this moment only
dreaming that he is sitting beside the fire. Since there is,
it seems, nothing in waking **experience** which is able to
distinguish a vivid dream that one is sitting by the fire
from the experience of actually sitting beside the fire, it
follows, concludes Descartes, that he is unable to know
that he is not presently in this dreaming state. Moreover,
given that if he was in such a dreaming state he would not
have the perceptual **knowledge** of his environment that he
could only have if he were awake, it also appears to follow
that he can't know that he is sitting by the fire. The hypothesis that one might be enjoying a vivid dream is thus
able to undermine one's putative knowledge of one's environment. For Descartes, this sceptical argument is part
of his general methodological strategy in **epistemology** of
doubting all that is not certain so that he can discover
the secure foundations for knowledge, but the argument
stands independently of this wider theoretical goal.

One further feature of the dreaming argument is worthy of note, which is that unlike most sceptical arguments in the contemporary debate it cannot obviously

be formulated in terms of the **closure principle**. This is because the hypothesis that one is dreaming is not inconsistent with the relevant class of one's everyday beliefs (in this case concerning the fact that one is sitting beside a fire), but only with one's knowledge of them. One could, after all, be sitting in one's armchair beside the fire and dreaming that one is sitting in one's armchair by the fire. Accordingly, insofar as one is able to form beliefs in one's sleep, then one's beliefs would be true, though intuitively they wouldn't amount to knowledge because of the way in which they were formed. **DHP**

See **closure, principle of; Descartes, René; scepticism**
Further reading: Stroud 1984, ch. 1

Dretske, Fred (1932–): An American philosopher who has made significant contributions to **epistemology**, many of which can be connected to his important critique of the **closure principle** for knowledge. Dretske has argued that, contrary to what is usually supposed, **knowledge** is not closed under known entailment by defending that in order for a subject to know a **proposition**, the subject must be able to eliminate only the **relevant alternatives** to that proposition (rather than *all* the alternatives to that proposition). If this is true, then one can know a proposition without knowing the falsity of all the (known) consequences of that proposition, which ultimately leads to a denial of closure. Dretske has supplemented his relevant alternatives theory – and his anti-closure argument – by developing and defending a modal condition for knowledge: the **sensitivity** condition. Dretske has also contributed to epistemology by proposing an **information**-based account of knowledge. **MB**

See **closure, principle of; contrastivism; information; modal epistemology; relevant alternatives; sensitivity**

Further reading: Dretske 1969, 1970, 1971, 1981, 2000; McLaughlin 1991

Dummett, Michael (1925–): British philosopher who has developed an influential version of **anti-realism**. Drawing on the philosophy of Frege, Dummett has argued that in order to explain language use one must identify how agents manifest their **knowledge** of the truth-conditions of the sentences they utter. Crucially, however, Dummett claims that the language use that is exhibited could be explained by positing a very weak anti-realist construal of the **truth** predicate. That is, one does not need to understand an agent's knowledge of truth-conditions by understanding the truth predicate in a robust non-epistemic fashion, such as in terms of a correspondence relation with the facts, for example. Instead, one could, argues Dummett, explain the language use manifested by understanding the truth predicate in merely epistemic terms, such as in terms of warranted assertion. An anti-realism thus emerges that is motivated by considerations in the philosophy of language. Such a view has been developed in recent years by **Wright. DHP**
See **realism/anti-realism; truth**
Further reading: Dummett 1978; Heck 1998

Empiricism: The key claim made by empiricist philosophers, and which sets them apart from exponents of **rationalism,** is that the only way something can be known to be real is, whether directly or indirectly, via **experience.** Historically, such a tradition is associated with the work of such figures as **Berkeley, Locke,** and **Hume,** though one can trace proto-empiricist thought right back into antiquity. In more recent philosophical debate versions of this general view have been advanced by **Mill**, **Russell**, Carnap, **Ayer**, **Quine**, **Dummett** and **Wright**. It is a characteristic feature of empiricism that it imposes fairly stringent constraints on what can count as known. Metaphysical, mathematical, religious, aesthetic, and ethical claims have all come under attack at one point or another by empiricists who have contended that such claims must be rejected on the grounds that they are not suitably related to experience. Indeed, even logical and philosophical **knowledge** can start to look dubious from the perspective of an empiricist philosophy, and this has been one of the main sources of dissatisfaction with the view.

One of the key ramifications of empiricism for **epistemology** is regarding our putative knowledge of the external world. After all, one might plausibly contend that all that experience gives us licence to believe in is the appearance of an external world, and not the external world itself. With this in mind, some, such as Berkeley, have seen in empiricism a motivation for **idealism**. Others, however, such as Hume, have employed empiricist considerations to draw straightforward sceptical conclusions regarding our knowledge of an external world (and much else besides, such as our knowledge gained via **induction**). DHP

See *a priori/a posteriori*; Berkeley, George; **Hume, David**; Locke, John; rationalism

Further reading: Woolhouse 1988; Garrett 1997; Atherton 1999

Empirical: see *a priori/a posteriori*

Epistemic blame: see **blame, epistemic**

Epistemic deflationism: see **deflationism, epistemic**

Epistemic deontologism: see **deontologism, epistemic**

Epistemic luck: see **luck, epistemic**

Epistemic norms: see **norms, epistemic**

Epistemic value: see **value, epistemic**

Epistemic virtue: see **intellectual virtue**

Epistemology: Also referred to as 'theory of **knowledge**', epistemology is the branch of philosophy that deals with issues surrounding (1) the nature of knowledge, (2) the sources of knowledge, and (3) the extent of knowledge. For the most part, epistemologists have been interested in **propositional knowledge**. Recently, however, there has been an increasing interest in **ability knowledge** and **interrogative knowledge** as well.

(1) primarily deals with the question of what propositional knowledge is. Suppose that we say that John knows that it rains, for instance; *what do we then mean to say?* This question is usually interpreted as a challenge to formulate the criteria that must be satisfied in order for a true **belief** to count as an instance of knowledge.

(2) primarily deals with the question of what the sources of propositional knowledge are. Some sources of knowledge are widely accepted (**perception,** reasoning, **testimony,** and **memory,** for instance), though there are, nonetheless, interesting questions about what these sources are exactly. Other sources of knowledge are more controversial, among them such sources as the *sensus divinitatis*. It is common to distinguish between sources of knowledge that *generate* knowledge (such as perception, reasoning and testimony), and sources of knowledge that do not generate but *retrieve* knowledge (such as memory).

(3) primarily deals with the question of how much we know. Most people, however, will accept that we know various ordinary empirical, mathematical, and *a priori* propositions. But do we also know ethical propositions (such as 'that murder is wrong') or religious propositions (such as 'that God exists')? If so, how? And if not, why not? Also, there are some powerful sceptical arguments that purport to show that we do not know ordinary empirical propositions, thus limiting the scope of our knowledge dramatically. Not many people, however, will accept the conclusion of those arguments.

In recent years, various new branches of epistemology have been developed that try to offer a new perspective on traditional epistemological problems, among them **feminist epistemology, naturalised epistemology** and **social epistemology. MB**

See **criterion, problem of the; feminist epistemology; Gettier cases; knowledge; memory; moral knowledge; naturalised epistemology; perception; religious epistemology; scepticism; social epistemology; testimony**

Further reading: BonJour 2002

Ethical knowledge: see **moral knowledge**

Evidence: The most familiar kind of evidence discussed in the literature that is relevant to **knowledge** is *propositional* evidence: we accept one **proposition** on the evidential basis of another proposition. Besides propositional evidence, there has also been mention in the literature of other types of evidence. **Reid,** for instance, talks about the evidence of the senses. And **Plantinga** talks about *impulsional* evidence (the inclination to believe something).

Intuitively, evidence is always such that it favours one proposition over (one or more) other propositions. One might take the seeing of an apple, for instance, to be evidence which favours the proposition that there is an apple before me over the proposition that there is an orange before me. But sceptical arguments proceed from the idea that our evidence cannot favour ordinary propositions (such as that I have hands) over known-to-be-incompatible sceptical propositions (such as that I am currently a **brain in a vat**). Accordingly, the sceptic will argue that we don't know the everyday propositions. Our evidence just isn't good enough.

Recently, there has also been attention for a contextual element in the notion of evidence. Neta, for instance, argues that what counts as evidence is a context-dependent matter. On his view, what the sceptic does is not raising the standards for knowledge – as some forms of **contextualism** suppose – but restricting what counts as evidence.

Finally, **Williamson** has argued against a phenomenal conception of evidence and defends that one's evidence is just what one knows. The ramifications of this claim are significant, especially for the problem of radical scepticism. **MB**

See **defeater; evidentialism; lottery paradox; underdetermination**

Further reading: Neta 2002; Plantinga 1993b

Evidentialism: The core idea of evidentialism is that in order for a **belief** to be justified so that it can be an instance of **knowledge,** the belief needs to be based on adequate **evidence**. Clifford is often alluded to as one of the foremost spokesman of evidentialism and evidentialism is defended nowadays by such figures as Conee and Feldman, who hold that whether a belief has epistemic **justification** is determined by the quality of the evidence that is available for that belief.

The important question is, of course, *what kind of evidence* is qualitatively good evidence? Different epistemologists may give different answers to this question. For instance, according to classical **foundationalism**, a belief is justified if and only if it is either a basic belief or a belief derived from a basic belief. The standard idea, however, seems to be that the only evidence that is qualitatively good evidence is evidence that we have reflective access to. Evidentialism is therefore closely connected with internalism. **MB**

See **Descartes, René; foundationalism; externalism/ internalism; Locke, John**

Further reading: Conee and Feldman 1985; 2004; Pritchard 2003

Evolutionary epistemology: Evolutionary **epistemology** belongs to the broader category of **naturalised epistemology**. The core tenet of evolutionary epistemology is to explain certain epistemological concepts in terms of evolutionary concepts. For instance, one idea in evolutionary epistemology is that evolution is responsible for how our **cognitive faculties** work. Another idea is that one can explain the reliability of our cognitive faculties in terms of natural selection. Recently, there also has been quite some interest in evolutionary explanations of religious beliefs. **MB**

See **naturalised epistemology**

Further reading: Campbell 1974

Experience: When it comes to perceptual **knowledge**, experiences are of crucial importance, though it is notoriously difficult to define what experiences are. In the vast literature on the subject, one distinction philosophers draw when defining the notion of 'experience' is that between the character of an experience and the content of an experience. If I have the experience of a giraffe, for instance, the content of this experience is *of a giraffe*. But this experience also has a certain 'feel': it feels a certain way to have the experience of a giraffe (and if feels different from, say, having the experience of a tiger). Another distinction that has been drawn is between sensuous experiences and non-sensuous experiences. Suppose, instance, that one is appeared to in a particular way and that one forms the **belief** that one sees a giraffe. In this case, there is sensuous experience of a giraffe. But there is also a non-sensuous experience involved, namely *that the belief that one sees a giraffe feels right*; it feels like the right belief in those particular circumstances. An important question with which epistemologists have been preoccupied is whether all knowledge is based on experience – as **empiricism** argues – or whether there is also knowledge that is not based on experience – as **rationalism** argues. **MB**

See **empiricism; phenomenalism; rationalism**

Further reading: Dretske 1995; Plantinga 1993b

Expert knowledge: There is a social division of labour in the way in which we acquire a great deal of our **knowledge**, in that specialist knowledge is often transmitted to us via experts. Discerning for oneself how best to diagnose a medical complaint would almost certainly be very risky, while acquiring the necessary training to eliminate this risk would be time-consuming and possibly beyond one's cognitive powers. Accordingly, when it comes to medical matters, as with many other topics, one relies on experts to gain the required knowledge.

Much of the discussion of the role of experts in the acquisition of knowledge takes place within the general debate regarding **testimony**, since it is usually through testimony that experts transmit their knowledge to us (at least where testimony is understood broadly to include such sources of information as, for example, textbooks). One of the specific problems that is raised by expert testimony concerns the appropriate weighting that should be accorded to the testimony of experts when they disagree (as in court cases when both the defence and the prosecution cite opposing 'expert' testimony in support of their cases). **DHP**

See **testimony**

Further reading: Goldman 2001

Explanation: Often one of the key purposes of gaining **knowledge** is to understand just *why* something is the case – that is, to offer an explanation. The problem posed by the notion of explanation, however, is that there doesn't seem to be a single thing that is at issue in the request for an explanation. For example, in asking someone why a car crash occurred, one could be seeking an explanation regarding the physics of the event (for example, that a moving object came into contact with a static object and so on), or an explanation in terms of the goals and beliefs of the agents involved (for example, that the one driver was trying to overtake another car in order to make up for lost time on the way to the station, but that the person in the car in front didn't notice this and so didn't leave enough space for the other driver to get by), or an explanation in terms of some other feature of the event. Indeed, explanation is quite often a contrastive notion, in that what we want to be told is why a certain event happened rather than another specified event (for example, why one's car is a complete wreck, like it has been in an accident, rather than being pristine as it was earlier on and as one expected it to be now).

An influential attempt to offer an account of explanation which avoids some of these ambiguities is the *deductive-nomological*, or *covering law*, account offered by **Hempel**. Hempel characterises explanation in terms of a deductive argument composed of a premise that states the relevant law(s) of nature and a further premise that sets out all the relevant facts involved in the event. The conclusion of the argument, which is the event to be explained, is meant to be accounted for by the fact that it is entailed by these two premises. For example, if it is a law of nature that untainted water boils at roughly 100 degrees centigrade, then this law, coupled with the fact that, amongst other things, the water was placed in a container at a temperature well above this level, would entail the boiling of the water. The event of the water boiling is, apparently, explained by this entailment from the relevant law of nature and the facts concerning the temperature of the water. Hempel also proposed an analogous model of explanation that dealt with statistical laws and which was, as a result, inductive (the so called *inductive-statistical* model).

There are, however, a number of problems with this model of explanation. To begin with, there is the practical problem of specifying all the relevant laws and facts specific to the situation. Even setting this difficulty to one side, however, further problems remain. Perhaps the most pressing of these is that there are cases that fit this model where the conclusion of the argument is clearly not the explanation that we require. For example, suppose that an agent ingests a poison which kills within an hour, and that an hour later the agent is dead, though not because of the poison but because, as it happens, she was hit by a car. In such a case we can construct a deductive-nomological explanation of why the agent died that makes no mention of the car accident, but only refers to the fact that (1) there is a law concerning how ingesting this poison leads to death within an hour, and (2) the agent ingested this poison. Intuitively, however, the poison has nothing to do with the agent's death, even though her death is indeed entailed by her consumption of the poison and the relevant law, since what explains her death is the car accident. **DHP**

See **abductive reasoning; Hempel, Carl Gustav; understanding**

Further reading: Achinstein 1983; Hempel 1965; Lipton 1991

Externalism, content: see **content externalism/internalism**

Externalism/internalism: One the key disputes in contemporary **epistemology** has been between proponents of externalist and internalist views. In the first instance, this debate is focused on the notion of **justification**, although it has important ramifications for other epistemic notions, such as **knowledge**. Standardly, internalist accounts of justification are characterised by their insistence on some kind of *access* requirement to the facts which determine justification, where the access in question is usually *a priori* access, construed relatively broadly (that is, so that it includes **introspection**, and perhaps also certain types of **memory** and inductive inference). For example, my justification for my perceptual **belief** that, say, there is a chair before me, will be determined by facts that are reflectively accessible to me, such as that it appears to me that there is a chair before me. In contrast, the characteristic feature of externalist accounts of justification – such as **reliabilism** – is that they allow certain facts to count as justification-determining even though they are not reflectively accessible to the subject. In the perceptual case, for example, a justification-determining fact could be that I have formed my belief in a reliable fashion.

Indeed, externalist accounts will typically allow that at least some beliefs can be justified even if the agent has no reflectively accessible grounds in favour of her belief at all, just so long as the belief is formed in the right (external) kind of way. The classic example that gets cited here is that of the **chicken sexer**, which is an agent who is exercising a highly reliable belief-forming trait in order to form a belief about the sex of the chicks before her, but who seems to lack any reflectively accessible grounds (any good ones at any rate) for believing what she does. If one's intuition is that this agent's belief is justified, then one is siding with the externalist, whilst if one's intuition is that this belief isn't justified, then one is siding with the internalist.

The externalist/internalist distinction is usually applied to the concept of knowledge via the further issue of whether an internalist conception of justification is necessary for knowledge. Internalists tend to insist on this condition whilst externalists tend to resist it. **DHP**

See **chicken sexer; clairvoyance; iterativity, principle of; reliabilism**

Further reading: Kornblith 2001

F

Faculty reliabilism: Faculty or agent **reliabilism** is essentially a refinement of the basic process reliabilist thesis, as propounded by such figures as **Goldman**. One of the problems facing these early reliabilist views was that it seemed that unless some restriction was placed on the kinds of reliable process that can be **knowledge**-conducive, then one's **epistemology** would generate counterintuitive results. For example, one could imagine cases in which the reliability that is being exhibited is due to factors that have nothing to do with the agent (such as a case in which one forms one's **belief** about the heat of the room by looking at a broken thermometer, but where the belief-forming process is still reliable because whenever one looks at the thermometer the temperature of the room is automatically adjusted to conform to what the thermometer is displaying). The underlying thought behind faculty reliabilism is that what is needed to deal with this problem is a restriction of the belief-forming processes at issue such that only those processes that are stable features of the agent's cognitive character can count as knowledge-conducive. Thus, if the reliability is due to one's perceptual faculties, then it can be knowledge-conducive, while if it is instead due to some oddity in the environment, as in the thermometer case, then it won't count as knowledge-conducive. Various accounts of this sort have been offered, from the **proper functionalism** advanced by **Plantinga** which focuses on whether one's **cognitive faculties** are properly function-ing, to the **virtue epistemology** defended by **Sosa** which defines knowledge in terms of the appropriate exercise of one's **intellectual virtues** and cognitive faculties. Faculty reliabilism is, like process reliabilism, a form of epistemic **externalism**, and so faces problems that are common to all externalist theories. **DHP**

See **cognitive faculties; externalism/internalism; Plantinga, Alvin; proper functionalism; reliabilism; Sosa, Ernest; virtue epistemology**

Further reading: Greco 1999; Plantinga 1993b; Sosa 1991

Fake barn case: These types of cases are due to Ginet and have been used by **Goldman** to support a counterfactual analysis of **knowledge**. In the original case, Henry and his son are driving in the countryside and Henry points out various objects to his son in ideal circumstances (for example, in good light, with excellent eyesight): 'That is a cow', 'That is a tractor', 'That is a barn'. In this case, if Henry points towards a barn and believes that what he sees is a barn, we are inclined to say that Henry knows that the object is a barn. However, suppose that, unbeknownst to Henry and his son, the area they have just driven into is full of papier-mâché barns that look exactly like barns from the road. Henry and his son have not yet encountered such a facsimile barn and are just now looking at a real barn. Yet had Henry and his son encountered a facsimile barn, they would not have known that it was a facsimile barn, thinking that it was a real barn. In this case, if Henry believes that what he sees is a barn, we are inclined to say that Henry does not know that the object is a barn.

Goldman diagnoses our diverging judgements with respect to these two cases as supporting a counterfactual theory of knowledge, on which a subject knows a proposition only if the subject can eliminate all **relevant alternatives** to the target proposition. One interesting feature of the fake barn case is that it shows that environmental facts *of which the subject is unaware* can influence whether the subject knows or not. Thus, fake barn cases seem to support an externalist account of knowledge. Another interesting feature of this case is that it seems to make features of the context of the subject relevant to whether the subject knows or not. Thus, fake barn cases seem to lend support to a certain type of **contextualism** about knowledge. **MB**

See **contextualism; externalism/internalism; infallibility; infallibilism; relevant alternatives; scepticism**

Further reading: Gendler and Hawthorne (forthcoming); Goldman 1976

Fallibilism: A **proposition** or **belief** is fallible when there is a possibility that it might be wrong. Typically, the sense of 'possibility' here is an epistemic one, the idea being that one's belief, say, is fallible when, for all one knows, it is possible that it could be wrong (that is, there is an error-possibility that is not ruled out by the agent's evidence). Much of the interest in fallibilism in the contemporary literature is as a response to an **infallibilism**-based **scepticism** which demands that **knowledge** be infallible and therefore concludes (since we are infallible about very little, if anything) that we do not have the widespread knowledge that we think we have. In contrast, fallibilists maintain that knowledge does not impose this kind of austere demand.

A related issue in this regard is the relationship between fallibilism and the **principle of closure**, which demands (roughly) that if one knows one proposition, and knows that it entails a second proposition, then one also knows that second proposition. With this principle in play it seems to follow from one's knowledge of, say, the fact that one has two hands, that one also has knowledge of the denials of **sceptical hypotheses**, such as that one is a **brain in a vat**. The problem is that such sceptical scenarios are very hard, if not impossible, to rule out, and thus with closure in play the possession of 'ordinary' knowledge appears to make *extra*ordinary epistemic demands.

One response to this difficulty has been to marshal a fallibilist thesis by claiming that one can know an ordinary proposition, such as that one has two hands, without thereby having to know that one is not the victim of a sceptical hypothesis. Instead, all one needs to do is rule out the *relevant* error-possibilities, not also *ir*relevant sceptical error-possibilities. On the view that results, then – what is known as a **relevant alternatives** thesis – fallibilism leads directly to the denial of closure.

In contrast, some proponents of **contextualism**, such as **Lewis**, have argued that one can evade the sceptical problem with closure intact by 'contextualising' one's understanding of infallibilism. On this view the infallibilist claim that we must be able to rule out all error-possibilities is understood in such a way that the 'all' at issue here varies in scope in different contexts. The view that results is thus either a contextualised form of infallibilism or a species of fallibilism, depending on your perspective. **DHP**

See **certainty; closure, principle of; contextualism; infallibility; infallibilism; relevant alternatives; scepticism**

Further reading: Dretske 1970; Lewis 1996; Unger 1975

Feminist epistemology: A core idea in feminist **epistemology** is that epistemic concepts suffer from gender partiality: all important epistemic concepts are treated in a masculinised fashion. Furthermore, feminist epistemologists depart from the Cartesian tendency to locate **knowledge** solely in the mind of the subject and propose that the knower is 'embodied' instead. This gives rise to a completely different perspective on knowledge – a perspective on which, for instance, knowers are located in specific times and places.

Feminist epistemologies have been appearing in the literature since the 1980s, and there now is a vast number of different types of feminist epistemology available to choose from. Feminist epistemologies have offered new interpretations of such key epistemological concepts as **justification** and **rationality**, at the same time contributing new concepts and ideas to the epistemological discussion, such as the role of the community and of the emotions in the process of knowing. **MB**

See **social epistemology**

Further reading: Alcoff and Potter 1993; Haslanger 1995

First-person authority: Our **knowledge** of the contents of our own minds appears to be epistemically privileged, at least relative to other people's knowledge of our minds. For example, typically at least, if someone else wants to know what we're thinking then they will have to employ the **empirical** procedure of asking us and hoping that we speak truthfully in our response. In contrast, we can usually know what we're thinking simply by employing our non-empirical capacity of **introspection,** and we are able to gain more accurate beliefs in this regards as a result. There are exceptions to this of course, in that sometimes what we are thinking and feeling is clear for all to see (our embarrassment in a certain social situation, for example, could be manifest in our behaviour), and sometimes our self-deceit is such that others with special expertise or training, such as psychologists, may be in a better position to judge what we really feel or believe than we are. Nevertheless, these facts in themselves do not undermine the thought that, at least in general, our epistemic access to our own mental states is both different and superior to the epistemic access that other people have. This is what is known as first-person authority. **DHP**

See **introspection**

Further reading: Gallois 1996

Fogelin, Robert (1932–): American philosopher, most noted in **epistemology** for his work on historical figures such as **Wittgenstein, Hume** and **Berkeley,** and for his development of a view which he calls *neo-Pyrrhonian* scepticism, a variant on ancient **Pyrrhonian scepticism. DHP**

See **Pyrrhonian scepticism; scepticism**

Further reading: Fogelin 1980, 1994, 2001, 2003

Foley, Richard (1947–): An American philosopher, Foley has argued for a number of distinctive theses in **epistemology.** Two are particularly worthy of note. The first is his claim that the project of understanding such notions as justification and epistemic **rationality** should be treated as entirely distinct from the project of understanding **knowledge**. The second is his espousal of a conception of knowledge according to which knowledge is analysed in terms of true **belief** plus a further set of contextually-defined true beliefs – what has been referred to as a form of **epistemic deflationism**. DHP

See **deflationism, epistemic**

Further reading: Foley 1987, 1993, (forthcoming)

Foundationalism: Some beliefs are accepted on the basis of other beliefs. For instance, the **belief** that my roommate is out is based on the belief that his coat is missing. But is my belief that his coat is missing also based on a further belief? Perhaps on the belief that I *see* that his coat is missing. But is *this* belief based on a further belief as well? Furthermore, suppose that the belief that my roommate is out is justified. Presumably, the **justification** of this belief is due to its being based on the further justified belief that his coat is missing. But where does the justification of this latter belief come from? There seems to be a regress of justification, and the question then becomes: what is the result of this regress?

Answers to this question that have been proposed in the literature are (1) that the regress terminates with unjustified beliefs, (2) that the regress terminates with justified beliefs, (3) that the regress continues infinitely, and (4) that the regress circles back on itself. The foundationalist argues for the second answer: the regress terminates with justified beliefs.

More specifically, according to foundationalism the belief-chain terminates with a particular set of beliefs that are commonly called the properly **basic beliefs**: beliefs that are not based on the evidential basis of other beliefs and are justified without obtaining this justification from other beliefs. In sum, on foundationalism, beliefs can be justified in either one of two ways: either by being based on a belief that already is justified, or by being a properly basic belief. An enlightening metaphor used by **Sosa** to capture foundationalism, is the metaphor of the pyramid. Our body of **knowledge** is shaped just like a pyramid in that there is a broad foundation of basic beliefs that support all the other beliefs.

The most influential form of foundationalism is what has been called 'classical foundationalism', traces of which can be found in **Descartes**. The most notable claim of the classical foundationalist is that the objects of the basic beliefs are always indubitable or **self-evident,** propositions. Classical foundationalism has been subjected to severe criticisms, one of the most important due to **Plantinga**, who argues that classical foundationalism is self-referentially incoherent (it does not itself meet the criteria for justification that it proposes). **MB**

See **basic and non-basic belief; coherentism; foundherentism; infinitism**

Further reading: BonJour 1978; Plantinga 1993a, 1993b; Sosa 1980

Foundherentism: A proposal regarding the structure of **knowledge** and **justification** put forward by **Haack**. The view aims to incorporate key aspects of both **foundationalism** and **coherentism**. From the former it takes the thesis that **experience** makes a direct contribution to epistemic status, such that sometimes a **belief** can have sufficient positive epistemic support directly without appeal to other beliefs. From the latter it incorporates the claim that some forms of epistemic status are transferred from other beliefs, and thus allows for the possibility that a belief can have sufficient epistemic status purely in virtue of the indirect support that it gains from other beliefs.

The metaphor that Haack uses to illustrate this thesis is the crossword puzzle, where the clues (essential to the puzzle) stand for experiences. Sometimes a clue will directly point towards a certain answer, and this is the parallel of direct experience-based belief, the epistemic status for which rests upon no other belief that the agent holds. Often, however, choosing the right answer will involve a mix of weighing up possible answers that the clues point to and seeing which words fit with other answers that one has already entered into the grid. Similarly, the epistemic status of most of our beliefs involves not just the direct support offered by perceptual experience, but also the support of other beliefs that we hold. Indeed, it could be that we put an answer into the grid for the sole reason that it is the only word which fits with the letters found, even though we are unable to see quite how it relates to the clue. To cash out the analogy, this would be a case in which the epistemic status of a belief was entirely dependent upon other beliefs that one holds and thus not due to perceptual experience at all. **DHP**

See **coherentism; foundationalism; Haack, Susan**
Further reading: Haack 1993

Generality problem: According to **reliabilism**, concepts such as **knowledge** and **justification** should be defined in terms of the notion of reliability. One pressing problem for this position is the generality problem as introduced by Feldman. The idea behind this objection is to say that only *types* of processes can be reliable or unreliable: the process in question should be *repeatable* in order to be reliable and token-processes occur just once, and can therefore not be the sort of process we are looking for. But if the question is whether a given type of belief-forming process is reliable, which type in particular do we aim at? To illustrate, suppose that I believe that I am drinking a cup of coffee. This particular belief is generated by a token-process which is the instantiation of the following types of process: one that starts with a visual image and results in a belief; one that takes place on a Saturday; one that takes place at 8.45 a.m. on Saturday; and so on. But which of these types is the relevant one?

Feldman (1985) points out that there are two scenarios here. We could, first, characterise the relevant types very narrowly. This, however, will ultimately have the absurd consequence that all true beliefs are justified and all false beliefs unjustified. We could, second, characterise the relevant types very broadly. This, however, will ultimately lead to the unacceptable consequence that the conclusions of all inferences are equally justified or unjustified, since they will all be believed out of processes that are of the same relevant type. The generality problem is the problem of finding an account of types that avoids both extremes. **MB**

See **reliabilism**

Further reading: Alston 1995; Conee and Feldman 1998; Feldman 1985

Gettier cases: In a landmark article in the early 1960s, Gettier offered two counterexamples to the **tripartite definition of knowledge,** the view which holds that **knowledge** is composed of three parts – **truth, belief** and **justification.** In the first case, an agent, Smith, justifiably forms a belief that a second agent, Jones, will get the job that they are both going for, and also that Jones has ten coins in his pocket. Since he is justified in believing both these propositions, Smith also justifiably infers that the person who will get the job will have ten coins in his pocket. This inferred be-lief is, it turns out, true, but not in the manner that Smith expected. The reason for this is that it is *Smith* who gets the job and, unbeknownst to Smith, he has ten coins in his pocket just like Jones. In the second case, Smith is justified in believing the false **proposition** that Jones owns a Ford and thus justifiably infers, on this basis, that either Jones owns a Ford or Brown is in Barcelona, where the sec-ond disjunct is a proposition which Smith has no reason for thinking is true. As it happens, however, Brown is in Barcelona, and so Smith's inferred belief is true. In both cases, even though the resultant belief is both justified and true, it is not an instance of knowledge. Intuitively, the reason for this is that it is just a matter of luck that Smith gets it right in this respect.

Initial responses to the Gettier problem focused on the fact that in each case Smith is making an inference from a justified, but false, belief. This led to the sugges-tion that what needs to be added to the tripartite account is a 'no false lemmas' condition which ensures that the belief is not based on any false assumptions. There are two problems with this proposal. The first is that it is almost certainly unduly restrictive in that there may be false assumptions made in the acquisition of a belief that play an entirely incidental role and yet, by the lights of this thesis, the mere fact that they are false will suffice to destroy knowledge in this regard. Even if one could evade this difficulty, however, a more serious problem remains which is that one can construct a Gettier-style case where the agent makes no inference at all. One such example, offered by **Chisholm**, is that of an agent looking into a field and seeing what he believes is a sheep. He therefore immediately (that is, non-inferentially) forms the belief that there is a sheep in the field. Unfortunately, however, the agent is looking at a cardboard cut-out of a sheep. Nevertheless, a real sheep is standing behind the cut-out, and thus the agent's belief is true. As with all Gettier-style cases, however, while this belief is both true and justified, it is not a case of knowledge because of the luck involved.

A related proposal has been to argue that knowledge is justified true belief where there is no further true proposition which would have destroyed the agent's justification had he believed it. This deals with the Gettier and Gettier-style cases that we have just described in that in each case there is a true proposition which would have destroyed the agent's justification had he believed it (for example, in the two Gettier cases, these are the truths that (1) Smith has ten coins in his pocket, and (2) Brown is in Barcelona). The problem with this proposal is that there can be misleading **defeaters** which, were I to become aware of them, would undermine my justification even though, were I not to become aware of them, they would not undermine my knowledge. Imagine, for example, that I am conducting an experiment to determine the temperature of a chemical substance. Whilst conducting the readings, and unbeknownst to me, there is a brief fluctuation in the temperature gauge. Had I noticed this then I would have formed the belief that the gauge was malfunctioning and thus would not have trusted the result of the experiment. This defeater would have thereby undermined my knowledge of the temperature of the chemical by undermining my justification for my belief in this regard. Crucially, however, this fluctuation did not represent a malfunction on the part of the gauge at all, but was merely due to a momentary surge in the electric current. In fact, the gauge is a highly reliable indicator of temperature. It seems, then, that I can come to know the temperature of the substance by using this gauge, and thus that although my justification in this respect might well have been undermined by noticing the fluctuation, it is fortunate that I did not become aware of this since it is a *misleading* defeater.

Both the proposals just considered try to meet the challenge posed by Gettier by adding an additional condition to the tripartite definition of knowledge. In contrast, some proposals try to deal with the problem by doing away with the tripartite account altogether. On one such view, one meets the Gettier problem by imposing a modal condition for knowledge – known as the **sensitivity** condition – which demands not only that one believes the truth in the actual world, but also that one does not continue to believe the target proposition (via the same method) in the nearest possible world in which this proposition is false. So, for instance, in Chisholm's 'sheep' example the agent lacks knowledge because in the nearest possible world in which what he believes is false – that is, the world in which there is no sheep in the field – he will continue to believe that there is a sheep in the field via the same method (in this case perception). His belief is thus insensitive to falsity and hence not an instance of knowledge. Notice, however, that all talk of justification here has left the picture. **DHP**

See **defeater; justification; tripartite definition of knowledge**

Further reading: Gettier 1963; Shope 1983

Given, the: In essence, the given refers to what is most immediate in our apprehension of the content of sense-**experience**. Typically, it is understood in a way that one's beliefs about what is given enjoy an epistemic priority over other beliefs – especially beliefs regarding objects in a physical world. For example, one's **belief** that the world is, at this moment, appearing to one in such-and-such a way would be a belief in what is given, with other beliefs, such as regarding whether the world is in fact in such-and-such a way, of a less secure epistemic status (and possibly even owing their epistemic status to an inference from the corresponding belief in what is given). In its extreme form, the given is represented by **sense-data** – parcels of immediate non-world-involving experience the content of which we are infallible (or at least incorrigible) about.

Epistemology in the later part of the twentieth century was characterised by a number of attacks on the given, led most prominently by **Sellars**. He argued that we should abandon this conception of our epistemic relationship to the world and that this meant also abandoning the idea that there is a foundation for empirical **knowledge** in the way that classical **foundationalism** supposes. For Sellars, there can be no in principle epistemic priority of one's beliefs concerning one's immediate experiences over one's beliefs about the world in the way that (he claimed) classical foundationalism imagines. **DHP**

See **experience; incorrigibility; infallibility; perception; Sellars, Wilfrid**

Further reading: McDowell 1994; Sellars 1997

Goldman, Alvin (1938–): Influential American philosopher most noted for his defence of an externalist theory of **knowledge** and **justification** known as **reliabilism**, and for his defence of epistemic **externalism** in general. Throughout his career, Goldman has tried to create links with the cognitive sciences, and one could regard his work as being one way of working through a **naturalised epistemology**. In recent work Goldman has worked on issues in social and applied epistemology. **DHP**

See **causal theory of knowledge; externalism/ internalism; reliabilism; social epistemology**

Further reading: Goldman 1986, 1992, 2001, 2002

Grice, Paul (1913–88): An American philosopher, it is Grice's work on the philosophy of language, and on pragmatics in particular, that has been most influential. Nevertheless, he did make a distinctive contribution to the epistemological debate regarding **perception**, offering a causal account. Moreover, his work on pragmatics has ramifications for a number of areas of **epistemology**. For example, Grice showed that one could account for the inappropriateness of certain assertions not by regarding what is said by these assertions as being false, but by treating the assertion as generating conversational implicatures which are false. In this way, a literally true assertion can seem false because in the context in which it was made it implied something false. One consequence of such a position is that it poses a standing challenge to **contextualism** in epistemology since this view tends immediately to infer from the fact that certain assertions are contextually inappropriate that what is said by these assertions is, in that context, false. In general, Grecian pragmatics has important implications for the conditions under which it is appropriate to claim **knowledge. DHP**

See **knowledge assertions**

Further reading: Grice 1989

Grue: see **induction**

Haack, Susan (1945–): A British philosopher, though one who has spent a good deal of her career working in the USA, Haack is most widely known for her defence of a distinctive proposal regarding the structure of **knowledge** and **justification** called **foundherentism**. Essentially, this is a view that incorporates key features of **foundationalism**

and **coherentism**. Haack has also been prominent in her attacks on **relativism** and on certain forms of **feminist epistemology**. DHP

See **foundherentism**

Further reading: Haack 1993

Habermas, Jurgen (1929–): A German philosopher and sociologist, Habermas is more widely known for his contribution to political theory than to **epistemology**. Nevertheless, his work does have ramifications in this area. In particular, his theory of communication incorporates an anti-realist conception of **truth** which understands truth in terms of consensus. On this view, a statement is true if and only if it would be accepted by all in what Habermas calls an ideal speech situation. Despite being committed to a form of **anti-realism**, Habermas has also been prominent in his attacks on **relativism**. DHP

See **anti-realism; relativism; truth**

Further reading: Habermas 1971, 1984–7; White 1995

Hempel, Carl Gustav (1905–97): A German philosopher, Hempel spent much of his working life in the USA, and is most remembered for his pioneering contribution to the topic of scientific **explanation**. In particular, the deductive-nomological model of explanation that he proposed, which understands explanation in terms of a deductive entailment from a law (or set of laws) and a description of the relevant antecedent conditions, is still widely discussed today. DHP

See **explanation**

Further reading: Hempel 1965

Higher-order beliefs: If one believes a **proposition**, should one then also believe that one believes that proposition?

That is, should one have higher-order beliefs about one's first-order beliefs? Not many people will answer this question affirmatively because it quickly leads to an infinite regress of higher-order beliefs. One instance in **epistemology** where higher-order beliefs are discussed is the **externalism/internalism** debate. **Alston**, for instance, has argued that internalism is committed to the position that for a belief to have internalist **justification**, the believer must be in a position to tell what the justifiers are. Since, Alston argues, this is a requirement that not many people will be able to meet, it should be abandoned, and the same goes for internalism. Conee and Feldman have recently defended internalism against this attack. **MB**

See **belief; externalism/internalism; higher-order knowledge; iterativity, principle of**

Further reading: Alston 1986; Conee and Feldman 2001

Higher-order knowledge: If one knows a **proposition**, does one then also know that one knows that proposition? That is, does **knowledge** of a proposition imply higher-order knowledge? The principle that says that higher-order knowledge is implied, is usually referred to as the **principle of iterativity**. Not many people find this principle convincing nowadays. One reason is that if it is true then it seems that small children and animals do not know anything since they do not know what knowledge is. Also, this principle seems to give rise to an infinite regress. For if one is to know that one knows in order to know, one also needs to know that one knows that one knows, and so on. **MB**

See **higher-order beliefs; iterativity, principle of**

Further reading: Alston 1980; Hintikka 1962

Highest common factor: It is commonly supposed that the content of one's perceptual **experience** is determined by what is phenomenally available to one. For example, if two people have perceptual experiences which are phenomenally identical then it follows, according to this conception of perceptual experience, that they are having the same perceptual experience. A good example to illustrate this view is the **brain in a vat** scenario often cited in discussions of **scepticism**. Here we are meant to imagine an agent who is having the same experiences as he would have had were he not a brain in a vat, but whose experiences are generated artificially rather than through normal causal interaction with his environment. It is thus supposed that there can be two cases, one in which an agent is being radically deceived and one where an agent isn't being deceived, where the agents concerned are having exactly the same experiences. **McDowell** has described such a view of perceptual experience as the highest common factor view, and argued that it is false. Instead, he contends that the content of one's experience is not exhausted by what is phenomenally available to the subject, such that a subject who is being radically deceived cannot have the same experiences as a counterpart subject who is not being deceived, even though there may be no phenomenal difference between each subject's experiences. The view that results is a form of **content externalism** that has ramifications for the problem of scepticism. Moreover, McDowell argues that rejecting this conception of perceptual experience is crucial if we are properly to account for the relationship between mind and world. **DHP**

See **content externalism/internalism; illusion, argument from; McDowell, John; perception**

Further reading: McDowell 1994

Hinge propositions: In his final notebooks, published as *On Certainty*, **Wittgenstein** undertook an extended discussion of the concepts of **knowledge** and **certainty**. In this discussion Wittgenstein argued that central to any account of these concepts is the notion of a hinge proposition. A hinge proposition is a **proposition** which has a special status in our epistemic practices, in that it cannot be coherently doubted or thought to be supported by further **evidence**. Crucially, however, the kinds of propositions that Wittgenstein had in mind here were very different from the sort of foundational propositions that are often thought to play this special role. In particular, the examples of hinge propositions that Wittgenstein cited – such as the proposition expressed by asserting the sentence 'I have two hands' in normal circumstances – are not obviously foundational propositions at all. That is, hinge propositions do not seem to be *self-justifying* in any way, which is what foundational propositions are often held to be, in that they are not, for example, **self-evident** or incorrigible. Nevertheless, Wittgenstein argues that such propositions cannot be regarded as supported by further evidence, in that any evidence which played this supporting role would have to be more certain than the proposition asserted, and there is no proposition more certain than a hinge proposition. Relatedly, there could be no coherent grounds to **doubt** a hinge proposition either, because any ground for doubt that was offered could not be more certain than the hinge proposition that was meant to be doubted.

Commentators have diverged over how best to understand Wittgenstein's thesis here. Some, such as **Wright**, have seen in Wittgenstein's remarks a basis for an anti-sceptical account of knowledge which allows that one can base one's knowledge on beliefs in hinge propositions which have an 'unearned warrant', in the sense that one can legitimately believe them even though they lack further epistemic support. Others, however, have seen in Wittgenstein's remarks in this regard an acceptance of some form of **scepticism**. DHP

See **certainty; incorrigibility; scepticism; Wittgenstein, Ludwig; Wright, Crispin**

Further reading: Wittgenstein 1969; Wright 1985, 1991a

Hintikka, Jaakko (1929–): A Finnish philosopher who has spent much of his life working in America, Hintikka has made a number of key contributions to **epistemology**, principally through his work on epistemic logic. In particular, he has developed a modal logic for **knowledge** and **belief** and used this model to cast light on a number of epistemological issues. At the heart of Hintikka's approach to epistemology is a conception of the appropriate methodology of knowledge acquisition which focuses on the role of questions and answers. This idea has been taken up in recent work in epistemology on **contrastivism**. DHP

See **contrastivism**

Further reading: Bodgan 1987; Hintikka 1962, 1974

Historical knowledge: The crucial epistemological question with respect to beliefs about the past is: can we be justified in believing these propositions? Can we, for instance, be justified in believing that the Battle of Hastings took place in 1066? The answer to the question whether our beliefs about the past can be justified depends, at least in part, on whether we know that the sources of our historical **knowledge** are reliable or trustworthy. We are not directly acquainted with the Battle of Hastings – we weren't there to witness it; our knowledge of this past event depends on various sources in which it is described. To the extent that these testimonial sources are known to be reliable or trustworthy, we can probably be said to have **justification** for **belief** in propositions about the past so that we can know these propositions. Moreover, some claim that with respect to some types of historical event, such as the occurrence of miracles, the reliability or trustworthiness of the testimonial sources should be very high in order for beliefs in the occurrence of those events to be justified. **MB**

See **memory; testimony**
Further reading: Coady 1992; Houston 1994

Hume, David (1711–76): Famous Scottish philosopher who belongs to the group of British empiricists. Hume has contributed to all areas of philosophy, and has put forward influential views on causation, ethics, miracles and personal identity. Central to Hume's epistemological thinking is the idea that **knowledge** and **belief** consist in having ideas, where all ideas are ultimately derived from impressions. In **epistemology**, Hume used his empiricist ideas to draw sceptical conclusions regarding our use of **induction** and our knowledge of an external world. **MB**

See **empiricism; Humean scepticism; induction**
Further reading: Hume 1989; Norton 1993

Humean scepticism: **Hume** is one of the best-known philosophers who proposed a form of **scepticism**. There are at least three important elements in Humean scepticism. A first important element is that this type of scepticism is motivated by considerations about the limits of **knowledge** based on **induction**. According to Hume, inductive arguments are never justifying and the central problem is how we can ever have a non-circular or non-question-begging **justification** for our use of it. Given that we use induction frequently in our daily reasoning, this position has important sceptical implications. Another important element of Humean scepticism is sometimes called his 'biperspectivalism'. Though Hume thought that there was no answer to scepticism, he nevertheless argued that sceptical doubts should be ignored when outside the study. A final important element of the Humean position is that we cannot help but believe that scepticism is false, even when presented with the most convincing sceptical argument. The reason for this is that Hume regards beliefs as a result of our natural impulses rather than as something regulated by reason. **MB**

See **induction; scepticism; Williams, Michael**

Further reading: Greco 2000; Hume 1989; Williams 1991

Hume's fork: 'Hume's fork' is used in **epistemology** to refer to the distinction between two types of **knowledge**: knowledge as a relation between ideas or else as about matters of fact. On **Hume**'s view, this distinction coincides with the distinction between *a priori* and *a posteriori* knowledge as well as with the distinction between **analytic** and **synthetic** propositions. Hume thus holds an opposite view from **Kant** who thought there are *synthetic a priori* judgements. **MB**

See **analytic/synthetic;** *a priori/a posteriori*

Further reading: Hume 1989

Idealism: A strand of thinking, usually associated with **Berkeley**, according to which everything in reality is mental or else depends on the mental. Idealism opposes materialism, according to which everything in reality is ultimately material in nature. A type of idealism that has been defended by **Kant** is transcendental idealism. Crucial in this view is the distinction between how things appear to us and how things are in themselves. On transcendental idealism, the categories of space and time represent the properties of things as they appear to us but they do not represent properties of things themselves. If idealism is true, then it seems that we can only know how the external world appears to us and not the external world itself. Thus idealism seems to lead straight into **scepticism**. MB

   See **empiricism; phenomenalism**
   Further reading: Langton 1998

Ignorance: Ignorance is the absence of **knowledge**. Ignorance is not a propositional attitude; one isn't ignorant *that it rains*, for instance. But one can be ignorant *about* what the weather conditions are. So ignorance usually applies to a particular subject-matter about which one lacks knowledge. Some people, most notably **Unger**, defend the extreme sceptical position that we are ignorant with respect to the external world: though we have many beliefs about the external world, and though these beliefs may well be true, they cannot be instances of knowledge. MB

   See **scepticism; Unger, Peter**
   Further reading: Unger 1975

Illusion, argument from: An argument, most commonly associated with **Ayer**, in favour of the so-called sense-datum theory of **perception**. It is familiar to most of us that things sometimes appear differently from what they are. One might perceive a red brick wall, for instance, whereas the brick wall is actually grey but illuminated by a red light. Or one might perceive a bent stick in the water, whereas the stick is actually straight. These are illusions. It is also familiar to most of us that we can sometimes perceive things that aren't there. One might – under the influence of some drug – perceive elves in one's room; the elves aren't there, of course – this is just a hallucination.

Now suppose that you perceive the red brick wall which is actually grey. In this case, what you perceive isn't identical to reality: the perceived red brick wall isn't identical to the real grey brick wall. Hence, what you perceive must be something mental, usually referred to as a sense-datum. In cases of illusion and hallucination, then, we perceive **sense-data**. But there is no phenomenological difference between instances of veridical perception and instances of non-veridical illusion or hallucination. Hence, what we perceive if our perception is veridical must also be sense-data. This is the argument from illusion. **MB**

See **perception; sense-data**

Further reading: Ayer 1947

Immediate knowledge: see **direct/indirect knowledge**

Imagination: The faculty of the imagination isn't usually seen as a source of **knowledge**. If I imagine that my car is red, do I then *know* that my car is red? It isn't obvious that the answer to this question is 'yes', even if it is true that my car is red. However, some philosophers do think that the imagination can be a source of modal knowledge. According to **Hume**, for instance, nothing we imagine is impossible. And for **Descartes**, the imagination can somehow help in acquiring **mathematical knowledge**. The ability to imagine mathematical shapes can help us in grasping certain mathematical truths. Recently, there has also been attention for what has been called 'the puzzle of imaginative resistance'. In short, this puzzle concerns the scope of what we are able to imagine, and shows that we are unable to imagine fictional worlds that we take to be morally deviant. Finally, there has also been some interest in the relation between **belief**, make-believe, and pretence, especially infused by experiments taken from empirical psychology. **MB**

See **belief; Descartes, René; Hume, David; mathematical knowledge**

Further reading: Gendler 2000; Gendler and Hawthorne 2002

Incorrigibility: A statement or **belief** is incorrigible when it is impossible that it might be refuted, corrected, or otherwise improved upon. Interest in incorrigibility in **epistemology** is largely with regard to our beliefs concerning our own immediate mental states, the idea being that no-one could be in a better position to judge what one is thinking or feeling than oneself (this view is sometimes known as **first-person authority**). Note that incorrigibility is a weaker notion than **infallibility**, which is concerned with the impossibility of being mistaken. It could be that one is mistaken in one's incorrigible beliefs, but that the beliefs in question are still incorrigible because no-one else is in a better position to find out the **truth** in this regard. **DHP**

See **first-person authority; introspection**

Further reading: Armstrong 1963

Indirect knowledge: see **direct/indirect knowledge**

Indubitability: To say that a statement or **belief** is indubitable is just to say that it cannot be subject to **doubt**. There are, however, nuances here regarding how one should construe the 'cannot' in play. After all, taken as a logical claim it is plausible to suppose that nothing is indubitable since anything could, as a matter of logic, be doubted. Accordingly, the idea is usually that an indubitable statement or belief is one that could not coherently or (stronger) consistently be doubted. A famous putative example in this regard – due to **Descartes** – concerns the **proposition** *I think therefore I am*, otherwise known as the *cogito*. Descartes argues that since only an existent thinker can think a thought, the mere fact that one is having a thought entails that one must exist. Accordingly, one cannot coherently doubt one's own existence, since the fact that one doubts this is itself a thought and it follows from one's having a thought that one must exist. There is a tight conceptual connection between such notions as indubitability, **infallibility** and **certainty**, in that a statement or belief that falls into one of these categories will tend to fall into the others as well, though it is far from uncontentious to say that these categories are co-extensive. **DHP**

See **doubt**

Further reading: Alston 1989, ch. 10

Induction: Perhaps the best way to define an inductive inference is negatively, as any inference which is not deductive – that is, any inference where the conclusion is not entailed by the premises. The main focus for discussions of induction in the epistemological literature has been on *enumerative induction*, which is where a generalisation is inferred from a set of instances of that generalisation. For example, one might infer from the fact that in a wide and representative sample of observed instances of swans all swans were white that, *simpliciter*, all swans are white. Clearly, the latter claim is not entailed by the former, since it is entirely possible that there might be unobserved swans which are, say, black. Nevertheless, intuitively at any rate, the premise does provide strong epistemic support for the conclusion. This form of induction needs to be separated from *hypothetical induction*, or **abductive reasoning** as it is known, where a hypothesis is inferred as being the best **explanation** available of the phenomenon in question. An example here could be reasoning from the fact that one's key no longer seems to work that someone has changed the locks, an inference that does not seem to rest at all on a set of relevant observed instances about keys and locks (not obviously at any rate).

The central problem directed at induction, usually attributed to **Hume,** concerns how one is to gain a non-circular **justification** for our use of it. The idea is that if we are to be justified in believing the conclusion of an inductive argument then it had better be the case that we have some justification for employing this style of inference. Crucially, however, this justification had better not itself make use of an inductive inference, since if this is the case then the justification will be question-begging. The problem is that it seems impossible to provide such a non-question-begging justification for our use of induction. We cannot, for example, appeal to the past success of inductive inferences and argue on this basis that we are justified in continuing to believe that they will be successful in the future, since this is itself an inductive inference. Given the importance of induction to the acquisition of knowledge, especially scientific knowledge, this argument has important sceptical implications.

A number of solutions have been proposed to this problem. One such suggestion, made by **Popper,** is that science does not actually employ induction at all, but a deductive system of inference known as *falsification*. This is where one makes a bold conjecture, such as that all swans are white, and then sets out to show it definitely to be false (for example, by finding a black swan, which would entail that the original hypothesis must be false). If this is right, then a lack of justification for induction would not undermine scientific **knowledge** at all. A very different proposal, made by **Reichenbach**, is to concede that there is no non-circular epistemic justification of induction available, but argue instead that there is a *pragmatic* justification for this form of inference. He compared the situation to that of a dying man who must choose between having an operation that he has no good reason to think will save his life and not having that operation which will *guarantee* that he will lose his life. In such a case, argued Reichenbach, the man would be pragmatically justified in having the operation even though he was not epistemically justified. The option to employ induction as opposed to not employing it is meant to enjoy a similar pragmatic justification.

A related problem associated with induction is Goodman's so-called 'new riddle' of induction. Goodman's puzzle concerns how we form a particular inductive conclusion on the basis of inductive premises rather than one of any number of alternative conclusions. For example, that all observed emeralds have been green is both evidence for the claim that all emeralds are green and evidence for the claim that all emeralds are 'grue', where 'grue' means green before a certain date in the future but blue thereafter. Although there are considerations that can be brought to bear here, such as the apparent simplicity of the former inference and the artificial nature of the predicate involved in the latter inference, it is not clear that these sorts of considerations should have any *epistemic* relevance to our inferences, being instead reflections of our subjective preferences rather than reflecting any epistemic grounds we might have to prefer the one conclusion over the other. Goodman's problem is closely related to **the problem of rule-following. DHP**

See **abductive reasoning; deduction; rule-following, the problem of**

Further reading: Goodman 1965; Holland et al. 1989; Popper 1963

Infallibilism: Infallibilism is an epistemological thesis largely associated with the early work of **Unger**. In essence, Unger claims that '**knowledge**' is an **absolute term** in the sense that it demands an absolute standard – in this case **infallibility**. (More specifically, Unger claims that knowledge entails **certainty**, and that 'certainty' is an absolute term, so the absoluteness of 'knowledge' is in this sense parasitic on the absoluteness of 'certainty'.) In this way 'knowledge' is held to be akin to other terms like 'empty' or 'flat'. The idea is that just as no surface is ever really, strictly speaking, flat (since there is no such thing as a frictionless plane), and just as no container is ever really, strictly speaking, empty (since there is no such thing as a vacuum), so nothing is ever really, strictly speaking, known. Unger explains our everyday use of knowledge ascriptions by comparing them to our everyday ascriptions of flatness to surfaces and emptiness to objects – ascriptions which merely reflect, he claims, rough-and-ready quotidian standards and which are thus not to be taken at face value.

If Unger is right, then this seems to entail a widespread **scepticism** since there are few, if any, beliefs which could plausibly be regarded as infallible. More recent work on infallibilism has tried to get around this problem while leaving most of Unger's key contentions intact by contextualising our understanding of infallibilism. On this view, most often associated with the work of **Lewis**, to say that a belief is infallible is not to say that it is immune to error *simpliciter*, but only that it is immune to error given the restricted range of error-possibilities at issue in that context. A form of **contextualism** about knowledge thus results. Moreover, Lewis claims that this approach can be extended to deal with our everyday use of other apparently 'absolute' terms, like 'flat' and 'empty'. Unger's recent statements on this topic are more sympathetic with this style of approach. He now claims that the linguistic data is ambivalent regarding whether it supports infallibilism or contextualism. Nevertheless, such ambivalence is still helpful to the sceptic, since it supports the second-order claim that we have just as much reason to be sceptics than not to be sceptics, and this also seems to license a form of scepticism. **DHP**

See **absolute term; infallibility; scepticism**

Further reading: Lewis 1996; Unger 1975, 1984

Infallibility: To say that a statement of **belief** is infallible is usually to say there is no possibility of it being mistaken or otherwise prone to error. It is thus a stronger notion than the related concept of **incorrigibility**, and bears some close conceptual connections with the concepts of **indubitability** and **certainty**. There are very few realms of thought, if any, in which we might plausibly claim infallibility, though two possibilities in this respect could be certain statements or beliefs in *a priori* realms like those of mathematics and logic, or certain statements of beliefs regarding our immediate mental states.

Following important work on this topic by **Unger**, recent interest in infallibility has tended to be concerned with its role in sceptical arguments, the thought being that **scepticism** gains at least some of its intuitive support from the fact that **knowledge** seems to be an infallible notion. In response, it has been argued – by, for example, **Lewis** – that we can make sense of a restricted or contextualist **infallibilism** in which a belief is infallible not in virtue of the impossibility of that belief being mistaken *simpliciter*, but rather in terms of the impossibility of that belief being mistaken within the restricted parameters defined by a context. DHP

See **infallibilism; scepticism**

Further reading: Lewis 1996; Unger 1975

Inference to the best explanation: see **abductive reasoning**

Infinitism: Infinitism is the view, associated with the work of **Klein**, that an infinite regress of grounds can indeed be **knowledge-** or **justification**-supporting, contrary to the conventional wisdom on this issue. If correct, this position could provide a novel way of resolving those problems in **epistemology** that turn on a regress argument, such as **Agrippa's trilemma.** DHP

See **Agrippa's trilemma; foundationalism; Klein, Peter**

Further reading: Klein 1998

Information: Information is typically understood in terms of **knowledge** which is stored, though not necessarily stored in the **memory** of an agent – as when we say that such-and-such information is available at the local library. In **epistemology,** however, a more specific use of this term has arisen which draws on the mathematical theory of information (what is known as *communication theory*). This understands information along statistical lines in terms of the relationship between events occurring at a source of information and events occurring at the relevant receiver of information. Part of the attraction of understanding epistemological problems in information-theoretic terms is that it seems able to offer a **naturalised epistemology** which dispenses with such normative notions as justification. The foremost exponent of an information-theoretic epistemology is **Dretske**. **DHP**

    See **Dretske, Fred; naturalised epistemology**

    Further reading: Dretske 1981

Intellectual virtues: The intellectual, or epistemic, virtues are those character traits of an agent that are conducive to the forming of true beliefs and, thereby, gaining **knowledge**. The character traits of being open-minded or conscientious could thus be regarded as intellectual virtues (though perhaps not exclusively: they may also be thought to be moral virtues). Although discussion of the intellectual virtues has always been a part of **epistemology**, in recent years it has come to the fore with the development of views known as **virtue epistemology** where the intellectual virtues take centre stage. For example, **Zagzebski** offers a broadly Aristotelian theory of knowledge which presents an integrated account of the moral and intellectual virtues in terms of the kind of character that an agent needs if she is to lead the good life. This is in contrast to the type of virtue-theoretic **reliabilism** proposed by **Sosa** who argues that an intellectual virtue might merely be a reliable cognitive faculty of the agent, such as the faculty of sight, and thus need not be part of the agent's intellectual character at all. **DHP**

    See **cognitive faculties; virtue epistemology**

    Further reading: Kvanvig 1992; Sosa 1985; Zagzebski 1996

Internalism, content: see **content externalism/internalism**

Internalism, epistemic: see **externalism/internalism**

Interrogative knowledge: One of the types of **knowledge** that hasn't received much discussion in the literature, though it clearly seems to be the one we use most in everyday language, is interrogative knowledge. Interrogative knowledge ascriptions are ascriptions of knowledge that use why/what/where/when/which/whether/who clauses, such as 'John knows where his car is parked', 'John knows who stole his bicycle', and 'John knows why he is late for work'. As some commentators have pointed out, interrogative knowledge is somehow related to questions. More specifically, it has been argued that if one possesses interrogative knowledge, one has the ability to answer a question. For instance, if John knows where his car is parked, then John has the ability to answer the question 'Where is your car parked?' An important topic of discussion is what the relation is between interrogative knowledge and **propositional knowledge**. In this respect, Schaffer has recently argued that propositional knowledge reduces to interrogative knowledge. **MB**

See **ability knowledge; Hintikka, Jaakko; propositional knowledge**

Further reading: Schaffer 2005c

Introspection: One introspects when one 'observes' the contents of one's own mind, such as one's thoughts. Observation of this sort (if observation is the right word) is very different from normal instances of observation which concern features of a world beyond the contents of one's mind, as when one observes that one's office door has swung open. For one thing, the latter sort of observation is straightforwardly **empirical**, while introspective observations seem to be *a priori*.

We often gain **knowledge** of the contents of our minds via introspection, as when we discover that we prefer action films to romantic comedies by reflecting on the different properties of films of each type. Moreover, it is often held that such 'internal' knowledge is epistemically privileged relative to normal observational knowledge.

For example, introspective knowledge is often thought to be incorrigible, in that while my judgements about how the world is can usually be improved upon (by using devices which enhance my vision for example), it is not obvious that my clear-headed and reflective judgements about what, say, I am thinking about right now can be improved upon. It is this sort of picture of introspective knowledge that has lead some epistemologists – known as *classical foundationalists* – to treat the foundations of our perceptual knowledge as being in part introspective. For example, while my empirical belief that there is a chair before me is clearly prone to error, it is not obvious that my belief that I am being appeared to as if there is a chair before me – something that I can know by introspecting my experiences – is prone to error, or at least prone to error to the same extent. Many have questioned this picture, however, citing recent work in psychology which suggests that we can be radically wrong in our introspective judgements, and even seems to imply that others, such as those with training in psychology, could be in a better position to make judgements about our mental states than ourselves, at least in certain cases. **DHP**

See **foundationalism; incorrigibility**

Further reading: Lyons 1988

Intuition: Most people will accept that we can know propositions like 'All bachelors are unmarried'. But what is the source of this *a priori* **knowledge**? The standard answer is that it is something like intuition. It is important to note that 'intuition' in this respect does not refer to some mysterious faculty – it simply refers to the fact that we can 'see' that a particular proposition is true. I can 'see' in this sense, for instance, that '1 + 1 equals 2' is true. Lots of work, obviously, goes into clarifying what intuitions are. Epistemologists have also argued that we can know moral propositions through the use of (moral) intuition. **MB**

See *a priori/a posteriori*; foundationalism

Further reading: BonJour 1998

Irrationality: see **rationality and irrationality**

Iterativity, principle of: In its simplest form, the principle of iterativity states that if one knows a **proposition**, then one knows that one knows this proposition. Though plausible (at least for certain types of **knowledge**), this principle does put quite a demanding constraint on knowledge possession, and this has made it contentious. In the recent epistemological debate a great deal of interest regarding this notion has been concerning its possible relevance for the **externalism/internalism** distinction in epistemology, since some have claimed that internalism, unlike externalism, demands acceptance of this notion. One problem facing this principle is that it seems to license a never-ending ascent of knowledge iterations, such that first-order knowledge entails second-order knowledge, which in turn entails third-order knowledge, and so on ad infinitum.

There are also a number of 'sister' principles to the iterativity principle discussed in the literature, such as iterativity for **justification** (if one is justified in believing a proposition, then one is justified in believing that one is justified in believing that proposition) and for **belief** (if one believes a proposition, then one believes that one believes that proposition). There are also 'mixed' iterativity-style principles which incorporate features of these other principles, such as the principle that if one knows a proposition, then one is justified in believing that one knows this proposition, a principle which is also often thought to be a central feature of an internalist epistemology. **DHP**

See **externalism/internalism; higher-order belief; higher-order knowledge**

Further reading: Alston 1980; Chisholm 1982a; Hintikka 1962

J

James, William (1842–1910): American philosopher and psychologist, and one of the founding figures of the school of philosophy known as **pragmatism**. James argued for a pragmatist conception of **truth** that understood truth, at least in part, in terms of utility. In general, in philosophical matters James was an ardent exponent of **empiricism. DHP**

See **pragmatism**

Further reading: Bird 1987; James 1961, 1975a, 1975b, 1976

JTB analysis of knowledge: see **tripartite definition of knowledge**

Justification: The notion of justification is among the most central notions in **epistemology**. Many epistemologists hold that in order for a true **belief** to qualify as an instance of **knowledge**, the belief should at least be justified. As various commentators have remarked, the justification that epistemologists are interested in is of a very specific sort. They are not interested in, for example, the moral justification or religious justification one might have for a belief, but rather in *epistemic* justification.

What, then, is epistemic justification? This question is notoriously hard to answer, but there is at least some agreement about the fact that justification is either concerned with the fulfilment of one's epistemic duties (where a duty is epistemic if it concerns what we should do if we want to believe properly) or else is truth-conducive (meaning that if we have justification for a particular belief, that belief is likely to be true). There is wide agreement that justification *by itself* isn't sufficient for a belief to be an instance of knowledge. As Gettier (1963) showed in a very influential paper, it is possible for a true belief to be justified without the justified true belief qualifying as knowledge.

Various theories of the structure of epistemic justification are currently on the market. Some of them are foundationalist theories, others are coherentist theories, and still others are foundherentist theories. Finally, there also are contextualist theories. All of these theories, moreover, can be put in either an internalist or an externalist framework. **MB**

See **coherentism; deontologism, epistemic; externalism/internalism; foundationalism; foundherentism; Gettier cases**

Further reading: Annis 1978; BonJour 1985; Gettier 1963; Haack 1993; Lehrer 1974

Kant, Immanuel (1724–1804): One of the greatest modern philosophers, Kant has contributed to virtually all areas of philosophy. In **epistemology**, two of his contributions that stand out are concerned with *a priori* **knowledge** and with the distinction between appearances and things in themselves (*Dinge an sich*). As to the former, Kant defends that *a priori* knowledge is independent of **experience**, while at the same time allowing that some synthetic propositions can be known in an *a priori* way. This claim has fuelled an enormous controversy. As to the latter contribution, Kant defends that there is a distinction between how things appear to us and how things are in themselves. According to Kant, we have no epistemic access to how things are in themselves. This claim has also been the subject of great controversy, with some people worrying that it leads straight into **idealism. MB**

See **analytic/synthetic;** *a priori/a posteriori*; **idealism; mathematical knowledge**

Further reading: Kant 1998

Klein, Peter (1940–): American philosopher whose chief contribution to **epistemology** has been his work on **certainty** and **scepticism,** and his advocacy of a novel response to the regress problem. As regards the former, Klein's view has been distinctive in its internalist defence of the **principle of closure.** As regards the latter, Klein has defended a position known as **infinitism** which allows that infinite chains of grounds can be **knowledge-** and **justification-**supporting. **DHP**

See **closure, principle of; infinitism**

Further reading: Klein 1981, 1998

Knowing how: see **ability knowledge**

Knowing that: see **propositional knowledge**

Knowing that one knows: see **higher-order knowledge**

Knowing why/what/where/when/which/whether/who: see **interrogative knowledge**

Knowledge: The concept of knowledge is one of the central concepts studied in **epistemology,** together with concepts such as **justification, rationality,** and **warrant**. Most epistemologists assume that there are at least three types of knowledge: knowing how (**ability knowledge**), knowing that (**propositional knowledge**), and knowing why/what/where/when/which/whether/who (**interrogative knowledge**). Most of the focus in epistemology, though, has been on propositional knowledge. With respect to propositional knowledge, various sources have been identified, all having their own kinds of problems. Sources such as **perception**, reason, **memory** and **testimony** count as the most discussed sources, though there has also been attention for more 'obscure' sources such as the *sensus divinitatis*. MB

See **belief; coherentism; contextualism; externalism/ internalism; foundationalism; Gettier cases; justification; knowledge assertions; knowledge by acquaintance/knowledge by description; memory; perception; rationality; tripartite definition of knowledge; warrant**

Further reading: Shope 1983

Knowledge assertions: The conditions under which one can appropriately make assertions which ascribe **knowledge**, whether to oneself or others, are of obvious interest to epistemologists. For although it does not immediately follow from the fact that it is appropriate to make an **assertion** that what is asserted is true (or from the fact that it is inappropriate to make an assertion that what is asserted is false), one would intuitively expect a relatively tight correlation between the conditions under which one can properly ascribe knowledge and the conditions under which it is possessed.

There are, however, complications here. When it comes to ascriptions of knowledge to others, for example, the problem is that it is not just the epistemic standing of the agent to whom knowledge is being ascribed that is relevant but also the epistemic standing of the one who is ascribing knowledge. After all, it is at least typically the case that I can only properly ascribe knowledge of a **proposition** to another if I also know that proposition myself. There are also problems specific to self-ascriptions of knowledge. As many have noted, the conditions under which I might legitimately say that I know a proposition seem to be more demanding than the conditions under which such knowledge is possessed. One reason for this, as **Wittgenstein** noted, is that saying that one knows is quite a special speech act, one that usually implies a unique or privileged epistemic standing as regards the proposition claimed.

One way of explaining this fact might be via the knowledge account of assertion. On this view, propounded most recently by **Williamson**, the rule of assertion is that one should only assert what one knows. If this is right, then the appropriate conditions under which one might properly say that one knows are when one knows that one knows. Thus the conditions under which one might legitimately say that one knows are *prima facie* more demanding than the conditions under which one knows.

A final complication regarding knowledge assertions comes from proponents of **contextualism** who claim that 'knows' is a context-sensitive term. On this view, the conditions under which one has knowledge will fluctuate from context to context, and this will be reflected in the conditions under which one might legitimately ascribe such knowledge. Thus two agents who agree on all the relevant facts, but who are each in a different context which has a different epistemic standard, may make the same ascription of knowledge to a third agent who is in an entirely different context and yet one of them speak truly whilst the other falsely. **DHP**

See **assertion; contextualism**

Further reading: DeRose 2002; Williamson 1996b; Wittgenstein 1969

Knowledge by acquaintance/knowledge by description: A distinction introduced by **Russell**. If one knows an object by description, then one knows that the object in question conforms to a particular description. I know the Queen of Denmark in this sense, for instance. Though I have never met her, I know her in the sense that I know what description she conforms to. One knows an object by acquaintance, however, if one is (or has been) directly aware of the object, without intermediary processes having been in play. Standard examples of things with which we are acquainted are mental states, such as the mental state of being in pain. The distinction between **knowledge** by acquaintance and knowledge by description is important in discussions about radical **scepticism**, because we might doubt that we are ever acquainted with objects. I would believe that I see hands (upon looking at them), for instance, even if I were currently dreaming of seeing hands and even if I were currently deceived into believing that I currently see hands. But if that is the case, how can I say that I am directly acquainted with my hands? Generalising on this, it is hard to defend that we are directly acquainted with physical objects at all. **MB**

See **scepticism; sense data**

Further reading: Russell 1912

L

Lehrer, Keith (1936–): An influential American philosopher, Lehrer is perhaps best known for his defence of a version of **coherentism** and for his work on the epistemology of **Reid**. Elsewhere in epistemology he has defended a distinctive resolution to the **Gettier cases,** and has been prominent in a number of disputes that are central to contemporary **epistemology,** such as the debate regarding the distinction between **belief** and **acceptance. DHP**

See **coherentism**

Further reading: Lehrer 1989, 1990a, 1990b, 1997; Olsson 2003

Lewis, David (1941–2001): Very influential American philosopher, Lewis is perhaps best known in **epistemology** for his defence of a version of epistemological **contextualism** that builds upon the **relevant alternatives** theory of **knowledge.** Key to Lewis's proposal is that in order for a subject to know a **proposition,** the subject must eliminate all alternatives in which that proposition is false, except for those alternatives that are in conflict with our proper presuppositions – and the conversational context will determine what those alternatives are. Lewis's contextualism is also a type of **modal epistemology** in that what is relevant for knowledge is the putative knower's relation to a (contextually determined) range of possible worlds. Lewis claims that his contextualism solves both the problem of **scepticism** as well as the **lottery paradox. MB**

See **contextualism; lottery paradox; modal epistemology; relevant alternatives; scepticism**

Further reading: Cohen 1998b; Lewis 1996; Schaffer 2001

Locke, John (1632–1704): Famous British philosopher who belongs to the school of **empiricism.** In his most famous work, *An Essay Concerning Human Understanding,* Locke defines **knowledge** as involving the **perception** of connections of agreement and disagreement between our ideas. According to Locke, our knowledge stems from **experience** – here he opposes the **rationalism** of Descartes.

Locke also allows for knowledge of religious propositions which can either be known by reason or by **revelation**. **MB**

See **empiricism; experience; primary/secondary qualities**

Further reading: Chappell 1994; Locke 1979

Lottery paradox: There are two interrelated puzzles that are referred to in the epistemological literature as lottery paradoxes. The first, due to Kyburg, concerns the following kind of case. Imagine a free lottery with long odds (the lottery involves, say, a million tickets, each with an equal chance of winning). Given the probabilities at issue, it would be rational to treat each individual ticket as being the losing ticket. But if that is right, then it seems to follow that it would also be rational to hold that *no* ticket will win the lottery, and yet we know this to be false.

A separate, though related, puzzle concerns the following two intuitions. The first is that if one bases one's **belief** that one has lost a lottery simply on the odds involved then that belief *cannot* qualify as **knowledge** (after all, for all one knows, one *could* have won). In contrast, if one bases one's belief on the report of the lottery numbers in the local newspaper (which is generally reliable regarding matters like this) then that belief *can* qualify as knowledge. What is puzzling about this is that the odds of the local newspaper being wrong are, intuitively at any rate, far greater than the odds that one will win the lottery. Accordingly, these two intuitions seem to entail the surprising consequence that knowledge is not a function of the strength of **evidence** that one has, where strength of evidence is, in turn, understood in terms of probabilities. **DHP**

See **evidence**

Further reading: Hawthorne 2004; Kyburg 1961; Lewis 1996

Luck, epistemic: It is often held that **knowledge** is, at the very least, true **belief** that is gained in a non-lucky fashion. Indeed, the classic counterexamples that are offered in **epistemology** – such as the **Gettier cases** – work precisely by showing that a true belief has met the rubric laid down by the target theory of knowledge and yet cannot be itself an instance of knowledge because of the luck involved. That said, very few commentators have *explicitly* defined knowledge in anti-luck terms. The two main exceptions in this regard are **Unger** and Pritchard. Unger has argued for a theory of knowledge in terms of non-accidental or non-lucky true belief, and has gone on to identify the specific sort of luck which is, he claims, incompatible with knowledge possession. Pritchard has extended this analysis, arguing that a number of different types of epistemological theories, such as **reliabilism, virtue epistemology** and **modal epistemology**, are best understood as ways of spelling out the idea that knowledge is, at root, non-lucky true belief. In particular, he argues that **safety**-based theories of knowledge are the best approximations to a pure anti-luck theory. Nevertheless, he also claims that there is a species of epistemic luck that is ineliminable by the lights of *any* theory of knowledge, and argues that the problem of **scepticism** plays upon our implicit recognition of this fact. DHP

See **modal epistemology**

Further reading: Pritchard 2005a; Unger 1968

Luminosity: In the work of **Williamson**, a luminous condition is one such that whenever it obtains it is known to obtain. Potential candidates for luminous conditions are one's immediate mental states, such as the feeling of being in pain. Plausibly, whenever I am in pain I know that I am in pain. Williamson argues, however, that no non-trivial condition is luminous, and this claim has a number of epistemological ramifications. For example, if no condition is luminous then it follows that one's beliefs about one's immediate mental states do not enjoy the kind of **infallibility** that one often ascribes to them. Moreover, the denial of luminosity also has implications for a number of epistemic principles, such as the **principle of iterativity** which states that if you know then you know that you know. If no condition is luminous, then it follows that the condition of having **knowledge** is not luminous either, and thus that iterativity must be false. **DHP**

See **infallibility**; **iterativity, principle of**

Further reading: Neta and Rohrbaugh 2004; Williamson 1996a

M

Mathematical knowledge: An important question concerning mathematical **knowledge** is whether it is *a priori* or *a posteriori*: is mathematical knowledge dependent on **experience** or not? **Kant** is probably the philosopher who has been most influential in shaping the debate concerning mathematical knowledge, and he famously argued that mathematical propositions cannot be known on the basis of experience. The reason is that, according to Kant, mathematical propositions are necessary, and one cannot know necessary propositions on the basis of experience. Another prominent position in the debate is inductivism. On inductivism, which is an empiricist position, mathematical propositions *can* be known on the basis of experience. On **Mill's** view, for instance, mathematical propositions can be known through inductive generalisations of earlier experiences. **MB**

See **analytic/synthetic**; *a priori/a posteriori*; **Kant, Immanuel**; **Mill, John Stuart**

Further reading: Kitcher 1983

McDowell, John (1942–): An influential British philosopher, though one who has spent much of his academic career in the USA. McDowell is most noted in **epistemology** for his work on perceptual **knowledge** and, in particular, for his development of an account of such knowledge which does not understand the content of perceptual **experience** along purely phenomenal lines. On this view, which is a form of content externalism, the content of one's perceptual experience in veridical cases is different from the content of one's perceptual experience in non-veridical cases (such as when one is the victim of a sceptical hypothesis), even though there may be nothing in the phenomenology of one's experience (that is, in the way in which the world appears to one) that indicates that one is in the one type of case rather than the other. Recognising this world-involving aspect of perceptual experience enables us, argues McDowell, to overcome the traditional philosophical problems that arise out of the old picture of the relationship between mind and world, such as the problem of **scepticism**.

McDowell has also argued for a number of related epistemological theses in this respect. For example, while he has argued that knowing is being in what he calls 'the space of reasons', a position which rules out certain forms of epistemic externalism which accord knowledge to agents who are unable to be moved by rational considerations, he nevertheless also claims that **reasons** can be factive – that is, that one's reason for believing a proposition can *entail* that proposition. The epistemology that results is thus traditional in its stress on the **rationality** of the agent, but also radical in that this rationality will typically manifest itself in a way that entails truths about the world. McDowell has also tried to transplant the general structural features of his approach to perceptual knowledge onto an account of other sources of knowledge, such as **testimony**. DHP

See **content externalism/internalism; externalism/ internalism; highest common factor; reasons; sceptical hypotheses**

Further reading: McDowell 1994, 2001a, 2001b; Smith 2002

Mediate knowledge: see **direct/indirect knowledge**

Memory: Much of what we know is stored in our memory and it seems natural to say that memory is a source of **knowledge**. We must be careful here, however, because unlike sources of knowledge like **perception** and reasoning that can *generate* knowledge, memory isn't capable of doing this; it can only retrieve knowledge.

When it comes to the crucial question of whether memory beliefs can be justified and, even, be instances of knowledge, every theory of knowledge will offer its own perspective. The most important fact to be determined, however, is whether the memory is a reliable source of beliefs. For if not, then knowledge on the basis of memory will be highly problematic. The chances of showing this are dim. First, because, as **Alston** has showed, demonstrating the reliability of every source of knowledge will be problematic: we cannot show that a particular source of knowledge is reliable without making use of that very source of knowledge. Second, the faculty of memory has been subjected to extensive psychological research and it has been shown by some studies that memory isn't as reliable as many think it is. **MB**

See **perception; testimony**

Further reading: Loftus 2003; Plantinga 1993b, ch. 3.

Mill, J. S. (1806–73): British philosopher belonging to the empiricist tradition. In **epistemology**, Mill has contributed to discussions about the existence of *a priori* **knowledge** and knowledge of other minds. As to the former, Mill defends an empirist and inductivist approach, holding that mathematical propositions are knowable through **experience**. As to the latter, Mill holds that we are led to believe in the existence of **other minds** by way of analogical arguments. **MB**

See **analogy, argument from; empiricism; mathematical knowledge; other minds**

Further reading: Skorupski 1998

Missed clues: A particular type of counterexample (put forward by Schaffer) to the **relevant alternatives** theory as defended by **Lewis**. Essentially, a missed clue case is a case in which a person sees but does not appreciate decisive **information**. It is argued that Lewis's theory rules that the subject knows in a missed clue case, whereas this is the intuitively incorrect result. **MB**

See **Lewis, David; relevant alternatives**

Further reading: Black 2003; Brueckner 2003; Lewis 1996; Schaffer 2001

Modal epistemology: Proponents of modal epistemological theories characterise the key concepts of **epistemology** (typically their focus is on **knowledge**) in terms of the responsiveness of the agent's **belief** in the target **proposition** across a specified range of possible worlds. Much of the impetus for analyses of this sort comes from work by **Nozick** in the early 1980s, although one can find elements of a modal epistemology in earlier work by **Armstrong, Dretske** and **Goldman**. Essentially, Nozick's claim is that we should understand knowledge in terms of true belief that meets two tracking conditions. The first, called a 'sensitivity' condition, demands that the agent would not believe the target proposition in the nearest possible worlds in which what is believed is false. The second condition demands that the agent would continue to believe the target proposition even if it remained true in a nearby possible world where circumstances are different. Such a position is held to have a number of advantages, including that it can deal with **Gettier cases,** and meet at least one version of the problem of **scepticism** by showing us what is wrong with the **closure principle.** More recent modal epistemological views have made use of the **safety** principle, which demands that one has a true belief which remains true across a range of nearby possible worlds in which the agent continues to believe the target proposition. Other recent theories, such as **contextualism,** have made use of a complex mix of safety- and sensitivity-type principles.

It has also been suggested that other theories of knowledge, such as **reliabilism,** are best thought of in modal epistemic terms, because the central notion at issue, in this case reliability, is itself a modal notion. Indeed, it has been argued by Pritchard that luck is a modal notion, and thus that provided we understand knowledge as non-lucky true belief then we are *obliged* to understand knowledge in a modal epistemic fashion, whether in terms of sensitivity, safety, reliability, or some other condition. **DHP**

See **luck, epistemic; safety; sensitivity; tracking**

Further reading: DeRose 1995; Nozick 1981; Pritchard 2005a; Sosa 1999a, 1999b

Moore, G. E. (1873–1958): An influential British philosopher, Moore is perhaps most noted in **epistemology** for his attempts – *contra* **idealism** and **scepticism** – to prove the existence of the external world and for his espousal of a **common sense** philosophy. Besides this, Moore has made some important observations about the propriety of assertions such as 'It is raining and I do not believe that it is raining' – what are known as *Moorean paradoxes*. The problem with such propositions is that though they can be true, they cannot be coherently asserted. **MB**

See **common sense; idealism; Moorean responses to scepticism; scepticism**

Further reading: de Almeida 2001; Moore 1925, 1939; Wittgenstein 1969

Moorean responses to scepticism: Moorean responses to **scepticism** are responses which, following a famous anti-sceptical argument by **Moore**, offer a particular **common sense** reaction to the sceptical problem. In essence, Moore's claim was that he clearly knew that he had two hands and thus, since if he has two hands then there must be an external world, that he also knew that there was an external world, *contra* proponents of scepticism and **idealism**. Moore admitted that he couldn't prove his premises, but noted that we do not normally demand proof in our premises before we allow them to stand. Moreover, he also claimed that he was at least as certain of the premises of his argument as he was of the premises of the sceptic's opposing argument.

In the recent debate regarding scepticism, Moorean anti-sceptical theories (or 'neo-Moorean' theories, as they are often known), all share with Moore's response to the sceptic the key claim that we are able to know the denials of **sceptical hypotheses**, though the focus is typically on such hypotheses as that one is a **brain in a vat**, rather than that there is no external world. This anti-sceptical move is significant because many epistemologists have argued that **knowledge** of this sort is impossible. There are two main ways in which commentators have tried to motivate a Moorean response of this sort. The first is to offer a form of **contextualism** which allows that we know such **propositions**, albeit only relative to the 'low' epistemic standards in operation in everyday contexts. This sort of view has been defended by, for example, **Cohen, DeRose** and **Lewis.** The second Moorean strategy is to adopt a theory of knowledge based on the **safety** principle, which is held to be compatible with such anti-sceptical knowledge. This kind of view has been defended by **Sosa,** amongst others. In both cases, one advantage to offering a Moorean response is that it holds out the possibility that one is able to meet the sceptical problem without having to deny the **closure principle.** In recent work, Pritchard has developed Sosa's Moorean anti-sceptical strategy by supplementing it with a number of key claims. These include embedding the safety principle within a general anti-luck theory of knowledge, offering an account of the propriety of knowledge claims which explains why claiming to know the denials of sceptical hypotheses is inappropriate even when what is claimed is true; and showing how this Moorean strategy is in fact licensed by a consistent construal of epistemic **externalism. DHP**

See **closure, principle of; contextualism; Moore, G. E.; safety; scepticism**

Further reading: DeRose 1995; Moore 1925, 1939; Nozick 1981; Pritchard 2002; Sosa 1999a

Moral knowledge: Can we have **knowledge** of moral truths? Can I know that murder is wrong, for instance? This is the central question in moral **epistemology.** There are three major positions with respect to this question. First, the position that states that we cannot have moral knowledge. This is the position usually called 'Humeanism'. (**Ayer** and Mackie stand out as two philosophers who defend a Humean position.) Second, the position that we can have moral knowledge through **reason**. This is the position usually called 'Kantianism'. (Rawls and Korsgaard stand out as two philosophers who defend a Kantian position.) Finally, a third position when it comes to the question of the possibility of moral knowledge is intuitionism. Intuitionists (like, for instance, Dancy) hold that moral beliefs are very much like ordinary perceptual beliefs, and can be justified in a similar way. Accordingly, moral beliefs can be justified non-inferentially. Intuitionism, therefore, finds a natural home in a foundationalist approach to the structure of knowledge. **MB**

See **foundationalism; intuition**

Further reading: Dancy 1993; Roeser 2002; Sinnott-Armstrong and Timmons 1995

Naturalised epistemology: Naturalised epistemological theories are characterised by their commitment to the idea that epistemological theorising should be viewed as closely tied to the kind of theorising that takes place in the cognitive sciences, such as psychology and linguistics. In this, naturalised epistemologists take their lead from a famous article by **Quine** in which he claimed that we should reject the traditional picture of epistemological theorising as being somehow above or at least distinct from theorising in the cognitive sciences. In effect, Quine viewed **epistemology** as simply an aspect of natural cognitive science more broadly.

One key problem facing proponents of naturalised epistemology is how to account for the apparent normativity of epistemic evaluation. That is, while the cognitive sciences are often thought merely to *describe* the cognitive practices by which we gain **knowledge**, epistemology is often understood as a normative discipline. **Reliabilism** is one contemporary theory of knowledge that is often understood as being an instance of naturalised epistemology. **DHP**

See **Quine, W. V. O.**

Further reading: Kornblith 1985, 2002; Quine 1969a

Necessity: see **contingent/necessary**

Non-basic belief: see **basic and non-basic belief**

Norms, epistemic: Epistemic norms are the rules or standards by which we epistemically evaluate beliefs. For example, we often criticise beliefs that are formed in ways that are not appropriately sensitive to the available **evidence,** and this has led some commentators to suggest that the rule to *proportion one's **belief** to the evidence that one has in favour of that belief* is an epistemic norm, although this is controversial. Any epistemological theory which analyses the key epistemic concepts like **justification** entirely in terms of whether the agent in question adheres to (or at least does not flout) the epistemic norms is known as a *deontological* theory, though such accounts have fallen out of favour in contemporary **epistemology.** Instead, the currently dominant view of epistemic norms is that they should play only a peripheral role in one's epistemological theory. Indeed, the view that a deontological conception of justification is not an essential component of **knowledge** is often thought to be a defining thesis of epistemological **externalism,** a sub-species of which is **naturalised epistemology. DHP**

See **deontologism, epistemic**

Further reading: Miller 1995; Pollock 1986, ch. 5

Nozick, Robert (1938–2002): American philosopher, most noted in epistemology for the **modal epistemology** that he developed and the related response to the problem of **scepticism** that he put forward. Central to Nozick's **epistemology** is the idea that to know is to have a true **belief** which 'tracks' the **truth** across a relevant class of possible worlds. Very roughly, this means that in the nearest possible worlds in which what one believes is false, one no longer believes it, and that in the nearest possible worlds in which circumstances are different but what one believes remains true, one continues to believe it. One consequence of this conception of **knowledge**, argues Nozick, is that the **principle of closure** must be denied. This is because on the Nozickean picture of knowledge one can have a belief which tracks the truth regarding one **proposition,** know that this proposition entails a second proposition, and yet fail to know that second proposition. In essence, the reason for this is that the possible worlds that are at issue as regards knowledge of the first proposition need not be the same class of worlds at issue as regards the second proposition. With closure denied, one influential sceptical argument which trades on this principle is therefore blocked. **DHP**

See **closure, principle of; modal epistemology; sensitivity; tracking**

Further reading: Luper-Foy 1987; Nozick 1981

Obligation, epistemic: see **deontologism, epistemic**

Observation/theory distinction: The distinction between observational statements and theoretical statements is notoriously tricky to draw, and this problem has been a central concern in debates in the philosophy of science. On the face of it, one might think that the problem could be resolved in a very straightforward fashion by saying that observational statements, unlike theoretical statements, simply concern observations. The issue becomes complicated, however, once one starts to think about what counts as an 'observation' in this respect. Presumably, observation here cannot include observations that are aided by technical instruments (including microscopes, telescopes and perhaps even ordinary spectacles), since the use of such instruments clearly presupposes theoretical information and expertise. Even completely unaided observations are controversial, however, since it is not implausible to suppose that we bring to bear further apparently theoretical **information** which informs our judgement. If there are bright lights shining on a wall, for example, then I may take myself to be observing a different colour from the one that is presented to me in this light.

The importance of this distinction to the philosophy of science relates to two key issues. The first concerns the fact that science is often thought to work by drawing bold theoretical claims from the relatively meagre observational data available to us. On this broadly empiricist model of scientific knowledge, theories are ultimately adjudicated by the extent of their 'fit' with the observational data. The second, and related, issue, concerns the role of unobservable entities in the **realism/anti-realism** debate in the philosophy of science. It is common for scientific theories to postulate such entities, though hard to see exactly how they should be understood without a clear grasp of an observation/theory distinction. Whereas anti-realists will tend to treat such entities with suspicion, as merely theoretical posits, realists will want to resist this and allow them a full ontological status. **DHP**

See **theory**

Further reading: Van Fraassen 1980

Omniscient interpreter: The case of the omniscient interpreter appears in a thought-experiment offered by **Davidson** to illustrate the anti-sceptical consequences of his use of the **principle of charity**. Davidson argues, in line with this principle, that it is in the nature of **belief** to be veridical, such that we could not make sense of an agent *qua* believer without also ascribing mostly true beliefs to that agent. Moreover, argues Davidson, even an interpreter with greater epistemic powers than ourselves, such as an interpreter who is omniscient about the world and about what does and would cause a speaker to assent to a sentence, would be no less constrained in her interpretation of that agent by the principle of charity. If this is right, then our interpretation of an agent's utterances, which treats that agent as having mostly true beliefs, are on a par in this regard with the interpretation offered by an omniscient interpreter who is offering the most 'objective' interpretation available of this agent. Thus, we can be assured that our treatment of agents – including ourselves – as having mostly true beliefs is entirely objective. In this way, Davidson aims to show that those forms of **scepticism** which turn on the possibility that most of our beliefs could be false are based on a false premise. **DHP**

See **charity, principle of; Davidson, Donald; scepticism**
Further reading: Davidson 1986

Other minds: Most of us think we know that there exist other minds besides our own. The problem of other minds is that this thought isn't as unproblematic as it might appear. For, first, we have direct access to our own mental states. But, second, we do not have direct access to the mental states of other persons. So, third, are we really justified in believing that other persons have other minds?

This argument, then, leads to a local variety of **scepticism**. There have been various responses to the problem of other minds. According to the behaviourist, for instance, there are no minds at all – there is only behaviour that we can observe. According to the **argument from analogy**, we can infer that other people have a mind by means of an analogical argument. Finally, the response of **verification-ism** to the problem of other minds is to say that the very idea of empirically inaccessible truths about others' mental states is incoherent. **MB**

See **analogy, argument from; Mill, J.S.; scepticism**
Further reading: Plantinga 1967

Past, knowledge of: see **historical knowledge**

Peirce, C. S. (1839–1914): American philosopher, and one of the founding figures in the school of philosophy known as **pragmatism**. Peirce argued for a form of **fallibilism** which he referred to as 'critical commonsensism'. This involved starting our enquiries not by doubting everything that can be doubted in order to find that which is most certain – which was the methodology recommended by **Descartes** – but by working outwards from our (defeasible) set of **common sense** beliefs. **DHP**

See **pragmatism**
Further reading: Hookway 1985; Peirce 1931–58

Perception: One of the basic sources of **knowledge** is perception. Indeed, it seems that without perception the only type of knowledge that is possible is *a priori* **knowledge**. There are two types of problem pertaining to perception.

The first type of problem concerns the nature of perceptual experiences: what are they? Two prominent answers that have been given in response to this question are the sense-datum theory and the adverbial theory. According to the sense-datum theory, what is given in perceptual **experience** are **sense-data**: non-physical, mind-dependent objects that we are directly aware of when we perceive things. According to the adverbial theory, what happens when we perceive something is that we are in a state of sensory awareness or, as it is commonly described, in a state of being appeared to in a certain way. The content of the perceptual experience can then be described by adding an adverb to the 'being appeared to' clause (for example, 'being appeared to redly').

The second type of problem concerns the question whether (and if so, how) we are justified in believing propositions that result from perception. Three prominent answers that have been given in response to this question are representationalism, **phenomenalism** and direct realism. According to representationalism, our perceptual experiences are representations of the external world. According to phenomenalism, physical objects are reducible to sense-data. Accordingly, if one believes to perceive a particular physical object, then one in fact believes in the existence of sense-data. Finally, according to direct realism, we have direct experiences of the physical objects we perceive – these direct experiences are not mediated by sense-data. **MB**

See **adverbial theories; phenomenalism; sense-data**

Further reading: Alston 1993b, 1999; Chisholm 1957

Phenomenalism: In its most austere form, phenomenalism is the view that physical objects are reducible to subjective sensory experiences, or **sense-data**. For example, on this view we should treat a physical object such as a chair as being reducible to our sensory experiences of chairs. In this way, our apparently epistemically problematic **knowledge** of the external world is made secure by tracing that knowledge back to our supposedly prior knowledge of how the world appears to us through our sense-data. Phenomenalism is a radical form of **empiricism**, in that it traces knowledge back to **experience**, albeit experience of a very restricted sort. **DHP**

See **empiricism; sense-data**

Further reading: Ayer 1946

Plantinga, Alvin (1932–): An American philosopher, most noted in **epistemology** for two contributions. First, for his defence of a new interpretation of the third condition for **knowledge**. Plantinga refers to this third condition as the 'warrant' condition, and argues that in order for a **belief** to be warranted, the belief should be produced by **cognitive faculties** that are functioning properly. Plantinga's theory of warrant bears a lot of resemblance to reliabilist and virtue epistemological treatments of knowledge. Second, for his defence of the thesis that religious beliefs can be instances of knowledge, because they can be produced by **cognitive faculties** that are functioning properly. Plantinga has also made many important contributions to metaphysics. **MB**

See **proper functionalism; reliabilism; religious epistemology; virtue epistemology; warrant**

Further reading: Kvanvig 1996; Plantinga 1993a, 1993b, 2000; Zagzebski 1996

Plato (427–347 BC): Plato is one of the founding fathers of modern western philosophy. In **epistemology**, Plato has proposed the idea – accepted by virtually all contemporary epistemologists – that **knowledge** is a form of **belief** – thus opposing a philosopher like Parmenides who thinks that knowledge and belief oppose each other. Also, Plato is important for having introduced (in the *Theatateus*) the standard, or tripartite, analysis of knowledge, on which knowledge is to be analysed as justified true belief. Finally, Plato has introduced (in the *Meno*) the idea that knowledge is more valuable than mere true belief: true beliefs are less stable and secure than are knowings. This last idea is currently receiving a lot of interest by virtue epistemologists. **MB**

See **tripartite definition of knowledge; virtue epistemology**

Further reading: Kvanvig 2003; Plato 1997

Pollock, John (1940–): American philosopher who has made an important contribution to discussions about such topics as **defeasibility** and **epistemic norms**. Pollock is also at work on epistemological problems surrounding artificial intelligence and rational decision making. **MB**

See **defeasibility; norms, epistemic**

Further reading: Pollock 1986

Popper, Karl (1902–94): Austrian philosopher who spent much of his academic career in Britain. Popper is chiefly remembered by epistemologists for his work on the philosophy of science and on the problem of **induction** in particular. Popper argued for a radical response to this problem by claiming that the growth of scientific knowledge is via a deductive method which he called 'falsification'. That is, it is a defining mark of genuine scientific theory for Popper (as opposed to what he considered were pseudo-scientific theories, like Marxism) that it entails bald conjectures which can be definitively tested and, if applicable, found to be clearly false. The idea is that while inductive **evidence** will always be limited in the support it offers, evidence which definitely disconfirms a theory will have a more unambiguous effect, completely ruling out that particular scientific conjecture. A number of problems face this view. To begin with there is the issue of whether any counterevidence will have the definitive effect on a conjecture that Popper supposes. After all, even fairly clearly-cut disconfirming evidence can be disputed (by querying the means by which it was acquired for example). Moreover, it is not clear where this approach leaves scientific knowledge, in that unfalsified conjectures on this view seem merely to have the status of provisional theses rather than knowledge (though, as a proponent of **fallibilism**, Popper may not have considered this consequence of his view a problem at all). **DHP**

See **induction**

Further reading: O'Hear 1980; Popper 1959, 1963, 1972, 1983

Pragmatism: Pragmatist philosophical views are typically characterised by their stress on practical utility. For example, one key pragmatist thesis has been regarding the theory of **truth**, where pragmatists have typically argued that since there can, they claim, be no practical difference between ideal **justification** and truth, so we shouldn't seek anything more from a **theory** of truth than a theory of ideal justification. In epistemology, pragmatist theories tend to be closely associated with **fallibilism** and the **naturalised epistemology** movement. The forefathers of pragmatism are generally thought to be **Peirce, Dewey** and **James.** Contemporary pragmatists include **Putnam, Rorty** and **Quine. DHP**

See **truth**

Further reading: Thayer 1982

Primary/secondary qualities: Very roughly, primary qualities are those features of objects that belong to the objects in their own right, whilst secondary qualities are those features of objects that are dependent upon human **observation**. For example, the shape of an object is plausibly a primary quality of an object, since it retains this property regardless of whether it is observed. The colour of an object, in contrast, appears to depend upon an observer and a set of environmental conditions. In **epistemology**, this distinction has been important to debates about the reality of the external world. **DHP**

See **idealism**

Further reading: Stroud 2002

Private language argument: An argument, supposedly due to **Wittgenstein**, which purports to show that the notion of a private language by which we name our **experiences** and sensations is incoherent. In essence, the idea is that many philosophical views implicitly incorporate the thesis that we, as it were, first assign a name to our sensations and experiences and then, subsequently, translate this private language into a public one by learning the correlating terms used in the public language. The core problem that Wittgenstein identifies with this picture is that without the constraints provided by the rules of communication that lie at the heart of a public language, there is no sense to the idea that private experiences could be assigned names. In short, the claim is that since there are no rules in play that would constrain a private language – and thus no way in which those rules can be misapplied – there is no sense to the idea that one can correctly apply a name to one's experience. **DHP**

See **rule-following, the problem of; Wittgenstein, Ludwig**

Further reading: Kripke 1982: Wittgenstein 1953

Process reliabilism: see **reliabilism**

Proper functionalism: Proper functionalism – as defended in the recent debate by, for example, **Plantinga** – is a form of **reliabilism** which is closely related to **virtue epistemology**. Proper functionalists claim that **knowledge** is essentially connected to the idea of an agent's **belief**-forming traits (including her **intellectual virtues** and **cognitive faculties**) properly and reliably functioning within an environment for which they are designed. Plantinga understands the notion of 'design' here in theistic terms, but this is not an essential part of the thesis. One could, for example, think of such design in broadly evolutionary terms as part of an **evolutionary epistemology**. DHP

See **Plantinga, Alvin; reliabilism; virtue epistemology**

Further reading: Plantinga 1993b

Proposition: A proposition is what is stated by a declarative sentence. For example, the sentence 'The cat is on the mat' states that something is the case, namely that the cat is on the mat, and this is the proposition expressed by this sentence. Note that the same proposition will be expressed by an analogue declarative sentence which is in a different language, such as French, just so long as what is stated by that sentence is the same. Propositions are truth-evaluable, in the sense that they can be evaluated as either true or false. DHP

See **propositional knowledge**

Further reading: Salmon and Soames 1989

Propositional knowledge: **Knowledge** can have different objects. One type of object, and the one that epistemologists have been concerned with most, is propositions. Propositional knowledge attributions assert that a specific sort of relation (that is, the *knowledge* relation) holds between a subject on the one hand, and a **proposition** on the other hand. Crucial questions with respect to the concept of propositional knowledge are what conditions need to be satisfied in order for the concept to obtain, and what the sources of propositional knowledge are. With respect to the first point, virtually all epistemologists hold that propositional knowledge is at least factive: to know a proposition implies that that proposition is true. With respect to the second point, widely recognised sources of knowledge are reason, **perception** and **testimony**. There has also been a lot of interest recently in how propositional knowledge relates to other types of knowledge, such as **ability knowledge** and **interrogative knowledge**. **MB**

See **ability knowledge; interrogative knowledge; knowledge; proposition**

Further reading: Ryle 1949

Putnam, Hilary (1926–): An influential American philosopher, Putnam's contribution to epistemological theorising has tended to arise out of his advocacy of a view that he calls 'internal realism'. One aspect of this view is the broadly pragmatist idea that it is incoherent to think of an ideally justified **theory** as being false (an idea which he thinks is a consequence of a thesis that he terms 'metaphysical realism'). Putnam thus advocates an antirealist conception of **truth**. A second characteristic thesis of Putnam's work, one which he also regards as being an element of his internal realism, is a certain form of **content externalism** which has ramifications for the problem of **scepticism**. Putnam argues that the content of a thought can be dependent upon the causal interactions that the agent thinking the thought has engaged in. In particular, he has argued that only someone who has appropriately causally engaged with water, or interacted with other members of a linguistic community who have appropriately causally engaged with water, can think water thoughts. Thus, an agent who has merely *seemed* to inter-act in either of these ways (that is, directly or indirectly) with water will not be able to think water thoughts. If this is right, then one consequence will be that an agent who has always been a **brain in a vat**, and who has not interacted with other agents who have causally engaged with vats, will not be able to think thoughts about vats. Thus, a brain in a vat who met these conditions would not be able even to think the thought that she is a brain in a vat (she would think a thought with a different con-tent instead). If this is right, then insofar as one really is thinking that one is a brain in a vat, then, necessarily, one cannot be a brain in a vat of this sort. **DHP**

See **brain in a vat; content externalism/internalism; scepticism**

Further reading: Clark and Hale 1995; Putnam 1981, 1983, 1987, 1989, 1992

Pyrrhonian scepticism: Most of what we know about Pyrrho-nian **scepticism** comes to us second-hand through the writings of Sextus Empiricus. This is no accident, in that one of the central claims of the Pyrrhonians was that one should not advance any philosophical thesis. In effect, Pyrrhonian scepticism consists of a series of *techniques* (rather than arguments as such) that under-mine any particular claim to know regarding a non-self-evident **truth**. The most famous of these techniques is probably **Agrippa's trilemma.** Unlike Cartesian scepti-cism, the goal of which is largely *methodological* (in that it is advanced in order to highlight something important, and anti-sceptical, about our knowledge), the goal of Pyrrhonian scepticism is a broadly *ethical* one. The Pyrrhonian sceptics claimed that by employing their scep-tical techniques which oppose 'dogmatic' claims to know, one would eventually achieve an entirely neutral attitude and outlook on life (*epoche*) which would ultimately lead to a tranquil and untroubled state of mind (*ataraxia*).

This ethical aspect of the thesis has been one source of controversy about the view, in that many have found it hard to understand how one can coherently 'live' one's scepticism in this way. The issue here turns on what counts as a 'non-self-evident' truth for the Pyrrhonians. If most of one's beliefs are of propositions which are non-self-evident, then it would indeed be problematic to think that one could suspend one's beliefs in such truths (although this may still coherently be an aspiration that one holds). In contrast, if what the Pyrrhonian sceptics had in mind when it comes to non-self-evident truths is simply theoretical or optional beliefs (as opposed, say, to basic perceptual beliefs), then the view starts to become more plausible. In the recent debate Pyrrhonian scepticism has once again been brought to the fore through discussion of the **underdetermination** principle and as a result of being defended in a modern form by such figures as **Fogelin**. DHP

See **Agrippa's trilemma; scepticism; underdetermination**

Further reading: Fogelin 1994; Sextus Empiricus 1933–49

Question-begging arguments: see **circular reasoning**

Quine, W. V. O. (1908–2000): One of the most influential American philosophers of the twentieth century, Quine has been closely involved with a number of movements which are important to **epistemology**. Chief among these has been his advocacy of **naturalised epistemology**, the view that epistemology should be regarded as, at root, merely a component part of the natural cognitive sciences, with no special normative status of its own. Quine also proposed a radical form of **coherentism**, one that allowed that *any* belief could be revised in the light of new **experiences**. Relatedly, he has argued against the idea of (apparently unrevisable) analytical truths – that is, truths that are true in virtue of their meaning alone. Quine's work is closely allied with the pragmatist school of philosophy. **DHP**

See **naturalised epistemology; pragmatism**

Further reading: Hookway 1988; Quine 1960, 1969b, 1973, 1981, 1990

Radical scepticism: see **scepticism**

Rationalism: The key claim made by rationalist philosophers, and what sets them apart from empiricist philosophers, is that an important part of what we can know to be real can be known to be real *independently of* **experience**. Historically, this tradition is associated with the work of such figures as **Descartes**. An example of a present-day rationalist would be **BonJour**. Rationalists crucially think that there are propositions that can be known only by **intuition** (for example, arithmetical truths). **MB**

See *a priori/a posteriori*; **experience**

Further reading: Descartes 1975

Rationality and irrationality: As has been remarked by various commentators, the concept of rationality – whether pertaining to decisions, strategies, intentions, beliefs, or still something else – essentially involves the notion of a goal. To say that a **belief** is rational, then, is to say that the belief will contribute to the achievement of a particular goal. And to say that a belief is irrational is to say that the belief will not contribute to the achievement of a particular goal. When it comes to rationality of beliefs, the goals will obviously be intellectual ones. **Foley,** for instance, holds that one intellectual goal that is important when evaluating whether a belief is rational, is the goal of having beliefs that are both accurate and comprehensive. One important discussion about the rationality of beliefs is whether the pragmatic consequences of a particular belief can make it rational or irrational to hold that belief. **MB**

See **Foley, Richard**

Further reading: Foley 1987, 2004; Lehrer 1999

Realism/anti-realism: Primarily, the realism/anti-realism debate in philosophy has been concerned with two interconnected issues. The first is the nature of **truth**. Whereas realists have tended to advance a conception of truth that understands this notion in terms of some sort of correspondence to the facts, anti-realists have tended to understand truth in epistemic or pragmatic terms, as being, for example, what we can be ideally justified in believing. The second key debate is concerned with the nature of reality itself, with realists insisting that the external world is something that is independent of our powers to cognise it, and anti-realists – such as proponents of **idealism** and **phenomenalism** – arguing that reality is in some sense dependent upon our cognition of it. Part of the attraction of anti-realist approaches is that it makes reality (and truth) something that is guaranteed to be accessible to us, since reality cannot outstrip our cognitive powers. As such, it offers one way of responding to the problem of

scepticism about the external world, which turns on the supposed potential epistemic inaccessibility of reality. In contrast, the enduring attraction of the rival realist view is precisely that it allows reality (and truth) to be more than what we think it to be.

Aside from this 'global' debate about realism and anti-realism, there are also a number of sub-debates which concern specific areas of philosophy. For example, although anti-realists in the philosophy of science will tend also to be anti-realists more generally, the specific concern in this area is with the putative existence of non-observable theoretical entities, as postulated by many scientific theories. Anti-realists will tend to want to say that such 'entities' do not really exist, with realists demurring. **DHP**

See **idealism; phenomenalism; truth**

Further reading: Brock and Mares 2005

Reason: see **rationality and irrationality**

Reasons: In epistemology, the term 'reason' is often used interchangeably with other epistemic terms like '**evidence**' or 'ground'. Clearly, however, this loose usage of the concept is misleading. After all, one's reason for believing a **proposition** could be a bad one, and in such a case it is far from obvious that this reason epistemically grounds one's belief, much less that it provides evidence for believing it. In general, the role of reasons is more often to explain the behaviour of agents – including the beliefs that they hold – rather than to account for the epistemic status of what they believe (though this is not to say, of course, that one's reasons aren't important to the epistemic status of one's beliefs).

One debate regarding reasons that has been important in contemporary **epistemology** has been whether to know is to be 'in the space of reasons', to use a phrase coined by **Sellars** and now employed by **McDowell** in his writings on the subject. If this is the case, then it means that the mere exercise of reliable cognitive traits will not suffice for **knowledge**, which is contrary to what a number of proponents of epistemological **externalism** have claimed.

A further issue that has been important to recent discussion of reasons has been whether it is possible for reasons to be *factive*, in the sense that the possession of a reason to believe a proposition entails the **truth** of that proposition. We certainly sometimes talk as if reasons can be factive, as when the reason we give for thinking that someone is in the room is that we can *see that* she is there (we can only see that something is the case if it is indeed the case). Nevertheless, many epistemologists have assumed that reasons cannot be factive in this way. This conventional wisdom in epistemology has, however, been challenged by McDowell, who argues for a version of **content externalism** that makes use of factive reasons and which, he claims, can help us resolve the age-old problem of **scepticism. DHP**

See **content externalism**

Further reading: McDowell 1994; Millar 1991

Regress scepticism: see **Agrippa's trilemma**

Reichenbach, Hans (1891–1953): German philosopher, most noted for his contribution to the philosophy of science and, in particular, for his work on probability theory and **induction**. As regards the latter, Reichenbach proposed a novel solution to the specific problem of induction posed by **Hume**. While he granted to Hume that there was no non-circular **justification** for our induction-based beliefs, he maintained that there was a pragmatic ground for accepting inductive conclusions (or at least for not doubting them all en masse at any rate). One of the examples he used to illustrate this was the dying man in the hospital who is told that without an operation he will die, but that the odds in favour of the operation succeeding were very low. Such a man should, if he is rational (and if saving his life is his aim), elect to have the operation, even despite the low chances of success, because the choice here is between guaranteed failure and possible success. In a similar way, Reichenbach argued that not to allow inductive inferences is to ensure predictive failure, while to employ them is at least to ensure the possibility of success. It is thus rational to employ induction, even despite the lack of a non-circular justification. **DHP**

See **induction**

Further reading: Reichenbach 1938, 1949; Salmon 1979

Reid, Thomas (1710–96): A Scottish philosopher and one of the founders of **common sense** philosophy, Reid is especially renowned for his criticism of the Lockean 'way of ideas' which is the theory that all mental phenomena are perceptions of ideas. On this theory, to think about a football means to perceive the idea of a 'football'. Reid argued that accepting this theory would lead straight into either **scepticism** or else **idealism** and defends a form of direct **realism** instead: we perceive the external world in a direct fashion which is not intermediated by ideas. In **epistemology**, Reid has defended an externalist theory of knowledge, as well as a form of **foundationalism**. Contemporary epistemologists who are strongly influenced by Reid include **Plantinga, Lehrer** and Wolterstorff. **MB**

See **common sense; externalism/internalism; foundationalism; Locke, John; Plantinga, Alvin**

Further reading: Cuneo and Van Woudenberg 2004; Lehrer 1989; Wolterstorff 2001

Relativism: Relativism is usually thought of as a view about **truth** to the effect that what counts as true is in some substantive way relative, whether to a socio-economic system, or to a particular agent, or some other parameter. So construed, the view faces an immediate problem, which is what to make of the truth of the statement of relativism itself. After all, if we treat this statement as relativised to, say, a particular social milieu, then it loses a lot of its interest, while if we don't then the view starts to look inconsistent.

A more plausible, though still controversial, way of spelling out relativist intuitions is to consider the application of the key epistemic concepts like **knowledge** and **justification** to be in some substantial way relative. Just such a view has been defended in the recent epistemological discussion by proponents of **contextualism** who claim that whether or not it is true to say that someone knows (or is justified in believing) a **proposition** can be a variable matter. That is, it is possible on this view that one person could claim that the agent concerned has knowledge while another person contends that the agent lacks knowledge, and yet both speak truly. Note that the claim is not that contradictory propositions can both be simultaneously true, which would be a very controversial thesis, but rather the less radical contention that 'know' is a context-sensitive term which picks out different epistemic standards when used by agents who occupy different epistemic contexts. **DHP**

See **contextualism; truth**

Further reading: Harre and Krausz 1995; Kirk 1999; Richards 2004

Relevant alternatives: In order to know a **proposition,** is it necessary that I rule out *every* possibility of error associated with that proposition? Intuitively, the answer to this is 'no', in that in everyday life we only demand that knowers rule out those error-possibilities that are in some sense relevant. For example, in order to know that the bird before me is a goldfinch, I may be required to be able to rule out that it is not some other bird that could be in the area just now, like a jackdaw, but we would not normally demand (at least not without special reasons) that I be able to rule out the possibility that it is not a mechanical goldfinch, made up to be an exact replica of the real thing. If this line of thought is right, then this prompts a relevant alternatives **theory** of **knowledge** which demands that one only needs to rule out *relevant* error-possibilities in order to know, not that one can rule out *all* error-possibilities, even irrelevant ones. Such a view would thus be a form of **fallibilism** which is directly opposed to **infallibilism**, and would thereby counter those versions of **scepticism** which are based on infallibilist considerations. One can find the beginnings of such a view in remarks by **Wittgenstein**, **Austin** and **Goldman**.

Nevertheless, simply denying infallibilism will not suffice for the relevant alternatives theorist to meet the problem of scepticism. This is because this problem can be motivated on grounds that are independent of infallibilist considerations and which instead appeal to the **closure principle**. Given that one is usually aware that one's everyday beliefs are inconsistent with the denials of **sceptical hypotheses**, this principle ensures that in order to know an everyday proposition, such as that one has two hands, it would be necessary also to know that one is not the victim of a sceptical hypothesis, such as the **brain in a vat** hypothesis, even though this error-possibility does seem to be irrelevant to our everyday knowledge.

Early versions of the relevant alternatives theory – as defended by **Dretske** and **Nozick** – responded to this difficulty by adopting a **modal epistemology** based around the

sensitivity principle which allowed them to reject the closure principle. Given the plausibility of the closure principle, however, this prompted some commentators to try to see if there was not another way in which one could account for one's relevant alternatives intuition whilst keeping closure intact. This led to the development of two very different theories of knowledge. The first, **contextualism,** in effect allows that the range of error-possibilities that are relevant to knowledge varies in line with contextual considerations, so that although one might know everyday and anti-sceptical propositions relative to the 'low' epistemic standards in play in everyday contexts, one knows neither set of propositions relative to the 'high' epistemic standards in play in contexts where the problem of scepticism is under consideration. Versions of this position have been advanced by **Cohen, DeRose** and **Lewis,** amongst others. In contrast, **Moorean responses to scepticism** simply argue that insofar as one knows everyday propositions then one also knows the denials of sceptical hypotheses that one knows to be inconsistent with these propositions. Such a view is still a variant on the relevant alternatives thesis in that it holds that the reason why one is able to know the denials of sceptical hypotheses is because the irrelevance of the error-possibilities that they concern means that one can have knowledge of their falsity very easily, simply in virtue of knowing everyday propositions and the relevant entailment. Such a view, which has been defended by **Sosa,** amongst others, often makes use of the **safety** principle. DHP

See **closure, principle of; contextualism; scepticism**

Further reading: Austin 1961a; Cohen 1991; Dretske 1970; Nozick 1981; Stine 1976

Reliabilism: Reliabilists hold that the key concepts of **epistemology,** and especially **knowledge** and **justification,**

should be defined in terms of the notion of reliability. So, for example, a justified **belief** will be one that is formed via a reliable process, where this means a process that leads to a greater number of true beliefs over false ones (this basic formulation of reliabilism is known as 'process reliabilism', as advocated in early work by **Goldman**). So understood, reliabilism tends to be associated with a **naturalised epistemology** and, more generally, with epistemological **externalism**, though neither commitment is obviously essential to the view.

There are a number of problems facing a basic form of **reliabilism**. To begin with, if the reliabilist holds that all there is to knowledge and justification is reliability, then they have to deal with such apparent **counterexamples** as the **chicken sexer** case, where the agent's beliefs are reliably formed even though she has no good reason to believe what she does, or the **clairvoyance** case in which an agent reliably forms true beliefs via clairvoyance even despite being in possession of counterevidence that should, intuitively, undermine the epistemic status of her belief. A very different difficulty is posed by the **generality problem** which queries on what basis one is to individuate the belief-forming processes at issue. If they are understood too narrowly, then it will be far too easy for a process to be deemed reliable and thereby knowledge-conducive; while if they are understood too broadly, then it will be almost impossible for a process to be deemed reliable, thereby preventing agents from gaining knowledge via this process.

Partly in response to problems of this sort, recent discussion in epistemology has seen the development of a number of different variations on the basic reliabilist thesis, such as **proper functionalism** and **virtue epistemology**. In each case the view is refined by, amongst other things, only allowing certain types of processes which are embedded in the cognitive character of an agent to count as knowledge-conducive. **DHP**

See **chicken sexer; clairvoyance; externalism/ internalism; generality problem; proper functionalism; virtue epistemology**

Further reading: Goldman 1986; Greco 1999; Plantinga 1993b; Sosa 1991

Religious epistemology: A distinctive branch of analytic epistemology that is interested in questions concerning the epistemic status of religious beliefs. These religious beliefs are for the most part beliefs like 'that God exists' or also more doctrinal beliefs like 'that God is triune' and most of the discussion takes place against the background of Christianity (which is not to say, of course, that similar questions do not exist for non-Christian religious beliefs).

One important project in religious **epistemology** is to investigate whether there are any arguments for the existence of God (the project of 'natural theology'). Here, Swinburne has developed an inductive Bayesian argument for the existence of God which purports to show that, given our total **evidence**, theism is more probable than not. Another important topic is whether (and if so, how) religious **experience** can provide religious **knowledge**. Here, **Alston** has argued that what he calls 'Christian mystical practice' can produce religious beliefs that are justified. Yet another important topic is presented by the so-called *reformed epistemologists*, among whom we can count **Plantinga, Alston** and Wolterstorff. Departing from a critique of classical **foundationalism** but accepting a form of foundationalism nonetheless, they argue that **belief** in God can be properly basic and, hence, be an instance of knowledge. Finally, a topic of considerable importance is the problem of religious diversity. Many people hold religious beliefs that are incompatible with Christian beliefs. But given this diversity, why could Christian beliefs be instances of knowledge, whereas Buddhist beliefs could not? **MB**

See **Alston, William; basic and non-basic belief; Bayesian epistemology; foundationalism; revelation**

Further reading: Alston 1991; Mavrodes 1970; Plantinga 2000; Swinburne 1979

Responsibility, epistemic: see **deontologism, epistemic**

Revelation: Religious **knowledge** can have a number of different sources. Two sources that have traditionally been recognised are **reason** and revelation. As to revelation, most commentators accept that at least two types of things can be revealed by God. First, God can reveal propositions, such as 'that I am triune'. Second, God can reveal himself (to a person). Philosophers have also distinguished between a number of different mechanisms by which God can reveal propositions. Mavrodes, for instance, proposes that God can reveal propositions by either manifesting them, communicating them (by divine speech), or by causing people to believe the proposition.

The big controversy in the epistemological literature on revelation is over whether, if a revelation has occurred, such a revelation can produce knowledge. Reformed epistemologists like **Plantinga** will argue that revelation can produce knowledge, presupposing that an externalist and foundationalist account of knowledge is true. Blaauw has recently argued that it is also possible to argue from an internalist account of knowledge that revelation can produce knowledge. Here, the idea is that knowledge is essentially a contrastive concept, and that changes in the contrast can affect whether a particular belief is an instance of knowledge or not. **MB**

See **Aquinas, Thomas; Plantinga, Alvin; religious epistemology**

Further reading: Blaauw 2004; Mavrodes 1988; Plantinga 2000; Swinburne 1992

Rorty, Richard (1931–): A prominent American philosopher, Rorty began his career working for the most part in the philosophy of mind, espousing a version of eliminative materialism. By the late 1970s, however, he had begun proposing the radical ideas for which he is now most well known. In essence, Rorty argues that apparently perennial philosophical problems are in fact the product of contingent historical developments. Accordingly, Rorty claims that philosophical puzzles are not the natural consequences of our concepts that they at first appear, but rather the result of *optional* features of our conceptual scheme. In general, Rorty lays the blame for a number of key epistemological problems, such as the problem of **scepticism**, at the door of a representationalist conception of the mental and the associated picture of the relationship between mind and world that goes with it. In this respect, Rorty agrees with **Sellars** that we must abandon the epistemological paradigm found in classical **foundationalism** and the myth of **the given** that goes with it. By rejecting such a picture, argues Rorty, we can avoid these age-old problems. In this way, Rorty's approach to epistemology can be viewed as a version of **epistemic deflationism**. Rorty's philosophy has often been accused of **relativism**, especially in its rejection of a correspondence conception of **truth**. It is certainly the case that Rorty is an adherent of **pragmatism** who thinks that utility should be a key goal of our enquiries. Nevertheless, as regards truth Rorty agrees with **Davidson** that truth should not be itself defined along pragmatist lines but rather treated as an indefinable primitive. **DHP**

See **deflationism, epistemic; pragmatism**

Further reading: Malachowski 2002; Rorty 1979, 1982, 1989, 1991

Rule-following, the problem of: The contemporary discussion of rule-following, and the putative problem associated with it, is largely in response to remarks made by **Wittgenstein** on this topic. Take the rule involved in adding two, as when one adds two and two together to get four. Part of Wittgenstein's concern about rule-following is what it is that enables us to know how to carry out this rule, given that it has an infinite number of instances (so it is not as if one learns the rule by learning all its instances). What if, for example, someone added two with numbers up to a thousand, but began adding four thereafter, claiming that she was following the same rule? Although we could point out the error, how are we to explain that such a rule must be continued as before indefinitely without presupposing prior knowledge of the rule? The contemporary treatment of this problem grew out of discussions of a related problem that Wittgenstein identified, known as the **private language argument,** which also raises issues about rule-following. **DHP**
See **private language argument**
Further reading: Kripke 1982; Wittgenstein 1953

Russell, Bertrand (1872–1970): A British philosopher who is best-known for his work in logic, and especially for his defence of logicism (that is, the view that mathematics can be reduced to logic), and for his theories of definite descriptions and logical atomism. In **epistemology**, one of Russell's most significant contributions is his discussion of the distinction between **knowledge by acquaintance** and **knowledge by description. MB**
See **knowledge by acquaintance/knowledge by description**
Further reading: Russell 1912

Ryle, Gilbert (1900–76): A British philosopher, Ryle is chiefly known for his defence of logical behaviourism, the position that the mental is not a part of physical objects. On this theory, physical objects have no hopes or fears, and to say that they do is to make a category mistake. In **epistemology**, one of the most significant contributions Ryle has made is to argue that there is a fundamental distinction between knowledge that (**propositional knowledge**) and knowledge how (**ability knowledge**). This position has recently been criticised by Stanley and **Williamson. MB**

See **ability knowledge; propositional knowledge**

Further reading: Ryle 1949; Stanley and Williamson 2001

S

Safety: A number of philosophers in the recent literature have argued that what is key to **knowledge** is that it is *safe*, in the sense that one's **belief** could not easily have been wrong. That is, safety is the claim that, roughly, insofar as one believes what one does then what one believes is true, and the idea is that satisfaction of such a principle is at least a necessary condition for knowledge possession. Expressed as a modal principle as part of a general **modal epistemology**, safety demands that if one knows then one not only has a true belief in the actual world, but also has a true belief (on the same basis) in the nearest possible worlds in which one continues to believe this proposition. So, for example, if one gains one's belief via an unreliable source then one will tend to fail to meet this principle, in that the unreliability of the source will usually mean that there is a nearest possible world in which one continues to believe the target proposition (and on the same basis as in the actual world) but where one's belief is false. Reliable sources of belief, in contrast, will tend to satisfy the safety principle.

One of the advantages of the safety principle is that it is weaker than the superficially similar **sensitivity** principle. In particular, while the latter principle is inconsistent with our knowledge of the denials of **sceptical hypotheses**, safety isn't. This holds out the promise that safety could form part of a response to **scepticism** that retains the **principle of closure** without adopting a form of **contextualism** – what is known as a **Moorean response to scepticism. DHP**

See **closure, principle of; modal epistemology; Moorean responses to scepticism; sensitivity; Sosa, Ernest; tracking**

Further reading: Pritchard 2002, 2005a; Sosa 1999a, 1999b; Williamson 2000

Sceptical hypotheses: The crucial way in Cartesian **scepticism** to introduce **doubt** is by introducing sceptical hypotheses. Well-known sceptical hypotheses are the dreaming hypothesis (it might be the case that the perceptual experiences that you now think you are having are mere dreamt experiences), the evil demon hypothesis (it might be the case that all the perceptual experiences that you now think you are having are put into your head by an evil demon), and the **brain in a vat** hypothesis (it might be the case that you are currently a brain floating in a vat of nutrient fluid, attached to a powerful computer that provides you with all the perceptual experiences you think you have). The evil demon and brain in a vat sceptical hypotheses are incompatible with ordinary experiences; we cannot both be seeing hands and be deceived by either the evil demon or the evil doctor. The dream hypothesis, by contrast, is not incompatible with ordinary **experience**; we can both dream that we are playing the piano while actually playing the piano. The important thing about sceptical hypotheses, some think, is that we cannot know them to be false. (How can we know that we are not a brain in a vat if the only way to determine this is on the basis of an experience which we would also have were we in fact a brain in a vat?) From this it then follows that we cannot know ordinary propositions either. (How can I know that I have hands if I cannot know that I am not a handless brain in a vat?) However, some epistemologists (most notably **Moore** and **Sosa**) think that we can know that sceptical hypotheses are false after all, thus providing a distinctive response to the sceptic. **MB**

See **Moore, G. E.; safety; scepticism; Sosa, Ernest**
Further reading: Putnam 1981; Sosa 1999a

Scepticism: The problem of scepticism is as old as philosophy itself. Generally, scepticism refers to the position that, with respect to a particular class of **beliefs**, those beliefs cannot be instances of **knowledge**. There are two types of scepticism to be distinguished. First, a local type of scepticism in which only a small part of our total set of beliefs (for example, religious beliefs, or beliefs about other minds) can never be an instance of knowledge. Second, a global type of scepticism. In global scepticism, a large part of our beliefs is said to be impossible to be instances of knowledge. For instance, it has been argued that we cannot know anything about the external world. It is especially the global variety of scepticism that many find absurd.

With respect to global scepticism, there are various important schools. First, there is the ancient **Pyrrhonian scepticism** (associated with the work of Sextus Empiricus). Pyrrhonian scepticism employs techniques instead of arguments in trying to undermine claims to know. Second, there is **Cartesian scepticism** (associated with the work of **Descartes**). Crucial in this type of scepticism is the use of sceptical hypotheses to cast doubt on much of what we ordinarily think to know. Third, there is **Humean scepticism** (associated with the work of **Hume**). This kind of scepticism is put up-and-running by considerations about the limits of inductive knowledge. Finally, an influential type of infallibilistic scepticism has been proposed by **Unger**. Unger proposes that knowledge is an **absolute term** that requires the elimination of all error-possibilities. Since this is impossible (we cannot eliminate sceptical scenarios), much of what we think to know isn't known at all. Much work in **epistemology** goes into answering these various kinds of scepticism. **MB**

See **absolute term; certainty; contextualism; contrastivism; Humean scepticism; infallibilism; Pyrrhonian scepticism; sceptical hypotheses**

Further reading: Fogelin 1994; Greco 2000; Unger 1975; Williams 1991

Secondary properties: see **primary/secondary qualities**

Self-evident: Propositions that are directly justified (for example, justified without being based on other propositions) are usually called self-evident. Examples of self-evident propositions are truths of logic and arithmetic, for instance: 'Every bachelor is unmarried' and '1 + 1 equals 2'. The term self-evident has also been reserved for those propositions that we cannot understand without automatically seeing that they are true. Self-evident propositions play an important role in foundationalist epistemologies in that they are usually seen as the propositions that are the foundation of our system of **knowledge** that carry the whole superstructure. **MB**

See *a priori/a posteriori*; **foundationalism; intuition**
Further reading: BonJour 1998

Self-knowledge: see **first-person authority; introspection**

Sellars, Wilfrid (1912–89): An influential American philosopher, Sellars is most noted for his attack on what he terms 'the myth of the given'. In its extreme form, the commitment to **the given** that Sellars is talking about here is represented by a **belief** in **sense-data** – parcels of immediate non-world-involving **experience** the content of which we are **infallible** about. Sellars's attack on the given goes well beyond attacking sense-datum theorists, however, since he argues that rejecting the given also means abandoning the idea that there is a foundation for empirical **knowledge** in the way that classical **foundationalism** supposes. For Sellars, there can be no in principle epistemic priority of one's beliefs concerning one's immediate experiences over one's beliefs about the world in the way that (he claims) classical foundationalism imagines. Another key theme in Sellars's work – one that has been taken up by **McDowell** – is the idea that epistemic discourse is irreducibly normative, in the sense that to have knowledge is thereby to be, as he puts it, 'in the space of reasons'. This identification of knowledge with rational considerations is in marked contrast to those epistemological theories which characterise knowledge in purely non-rational terms, such as certain species of **reliabilism. DHP**

See **given, the**
Further reading: Coates 2005; Sellars 1963

Sense-data: On the standard view, sense-data have two important characteristics. First, they are mind-dependent and, thus, cannot exist on their own. Second, in perceiving things, sense-data are the objects of which we have a direct awareness. For instance, if I perceive a red brick wall, then what I perceive isn't the red brick wall itself but the mental image of a red brick wall.

Various arguments in favour of the existence of sense-data have been proposed in the literature. Best-known in this regard is the **argument from illusion**. An important objection to the sense-data theory is that sense-data cannot be located in space. For if sense-data have the properties they appear to have, they must somehow have a location in space. But there is no clear answer to the question where in space they are located, which counts against the sense-data theory. **MB**

See **illusion, argument from; knowledge by acquaintance/knowledge by description; perception**

Further reading: Austin 1962a; Chisholm 1957

Sensitivity: The sensitivity requirement on **knowledge** (as proposed by **Dretske**) is a typical requirement that is made from the perspective of **modal epistemology**. Broadly, the sensitivity requirement says that in order for a subject to know a **proposition**, it is necessary that, were the proposition to be false, the subject wouldn't continue believing it. Put differently (and in the language of possible worlds): in order for a subject to know a proposition, the subject shouldn't continue to believe the proposition in the nearest possible worlds in which the proposition is false.

One important result of accepting sensitivity is that it leads to a violation of the **closure principle** for knowledge. Because if sensitivity is true, then one can know (1) that the animal in the pen is a zebra (one's **belief** that the animal in the pen is a zebra is sensitive: in the nearest possible world in which the animal in the pen is a tiger, one wouldn't continue to believe that the animal in the pen is a zebra); and (2) that if the animal in the pen is a zebra, then the animal in the pen is not a cleverly disguised mule; but fail to know (3) that the animal in the pen is not a cleverly disguised mule (one's belief that the animal in the pen is not a cleverly disguised mule is not sensitive: in the nearest possible in which the animal is a cleverly disguised mule, one would continue to believe that it was not a cleverly disguised mule).

But sensitivity is subject to a number of **counterexamples**. The most famous of these is the garbage chute case, proposed by **Sosa**. I throw a trash bag down the garbage chute of my apartment building. I come to believe that the trash bag is in the basement. However, in the closest possible world in which this belief is false, the bag is stuck in the chute. Now my belief that the trash bag is in the basement, even if true, is not sensitive: in the nearest possible world in which my belief is false, I continue to believe that the trash bag is stuck in the chute. Hence, on the sensitivity theory of knowledge, I do not know that the trash bag is in the basement, which seems to be the wrong result. Counterexamples such as the garbage chute case, have led some philosophers (for example, Sosa) to propose a closely related, but different, requirement on knowledge: the **safety** requirement. **MB**

See **closure, principle of**; **modal epistemology**; **safety**; **scepticism**; **tracking**

Further reading: DeRose 1995; Dretske 1971; Nozick 1981; Sosa 1999a

Sensus divinitatis: According to such reformed epistemologists as **Plantinga** and Wolterstorff, **belief** in religious propositions (such as 'that God exists') can be properly basic: these beliefs can be justified without being based on any other beliefs from which they derive **justification**. But what cognitive faculty produces such properly basic beliefs? Plantinga and Wolterstorff turn to Calvin where they find the idea of a special cognitive faculty that Calvin calls the *sensus divinitatis*. This faculty should be thought of as some sort of input-output device: in typical circumstances (such as beholding the starry heavens) which count as the input, the *sensus divinitatis* will produce beliefs about God. Some reformed epistemologists, such as Mavrodes, think of this procedure as a type of divine **revelation. MB**

See **basic and non-basic belief; cognitive faculties; Plantinga, Alvin; religious epistemology; revelation**

Further reading: Mavrodes 1988; Plantinga 1983, 2000; Zagzebski 1993

Sextus Empiricus: see **Pyrrhonian scepticism**

Social epistemology: A branch of **epistemology** that deals with the social nature of **knowledge, belief** and **justification.** The crucial idea in social epistemology is that epistemic conditions in some sense have a social nature: they are determined by communities of people. In this sense, social epistemology opposes much of traditional epistemology which holds that epistemic conditions can only be traced back to a knowing *subject.* In parting with the traditional epistemological framework, social epistemology resembles **feminist epistemology,** which also rejects an important assumption of traditional epistemology. Important topics in social epistemology are **testimony** and **expert knowledge. MB**

See **expert knowledge; feminist epistemology; testimony**

Further reading: Goldman 2002; Longino 1990

Sosa, Ernest (1940–): One of the most influential American philosophers working today, Sosa's impact on contemporary **epistemology** has been wide-ranging. He has consistently argued against key movements in epistemology such as **coherentism** and **epistemic internalism,** and has also been central to the current interest in **virtue epistemology,** maintaining a sophisticated version of this thesis himself. As regards the problem of **scepticism,** Sosa has tried to combine his virtue-theoretic approach to **knowledge** with a modal condition for knowledge – which he calls **safety** – in order to resurrect the **common sense** response to scepticism offered by **Moore.** According to this proposal, it is possible to know the denials of **sceptical hypotheses,** and thus one can evade the threat put forward by the sceptic without having either to deny the **principle of closure** or endorse **contextualism. DHP**

See **modal epistemology; Moorean responses to scepticism; reliabilism; safety; virtue epistemology**

Further reading: Greco 2004; Sosa 1991

Strawson, Peter (1919–): An influential British philosopher. Although the focus of Strawson's work has tended to be on metaphysics, he has made a number of key contributions to **epistemology.** One of the central themes in his work is a rejection of **scepticism,** whether scepticism in general or more local forms of scepticism that are focused on a specific target, in particular **induction** and **other minds.** As regards induction, Strawson argues that it is constitutive of **rationality** that one treats appropriate inductive inferences as rational. As regards scepticism in general, in his early work Strawson tried to advance a transcendental argument to the effect that scepticism is self-defeating because it attempts to make use of concepts which, by the sceptic's lights, are unintelligible. In his later work, however, he has argued instead that such radical sceptical arguments are idle in that they could never persuade us to change our beliefs in this regard. Very roughly, one can view the former style of response to scepticism as drawing from themes in **Kant,** while the latter style of response has more affinities with the work of **Hume** and **Wittgenstein. DHP**

See **induction; transcendental arguments; scepticism**
Further reading: Hahn 1998; Strawson 1959, 1967, 1985

Synthetic: see **analytic/synthetic**

Testimony: No one would dispute that much of our **knowledge** is dependent upon the word of others, and thus on testimony. It is therefore essential that we are able to offer a plausible account of the **epistemology** of testimony. In this regard there are two main schools of thought. On the one hand there are the *reductionists*, who take their lead from **Hume**. These commentators argue that the epistemic status of testimony-based beliefs needs to be ultimately reduced to non-testimony-based beliefs, such as observational beliefs. The idea is that without such a non-testimonial anchoring for our testimony-based beliefs we lack any good reason to hold that these beliefs are true. In short, the mere fact that someone testifies to you that *p* is not a reason to believe *p* – instead, you need further independent grounds in support of this **belief**. With the standards for testimonial **justification** set so high, however, one of the chief objections against this approach to the epistemology of testimony is that it appears to lead directly to **scepticism** about the epistemic status of most beliefs of this sort.

In contrast to the reductionists are the *credulists* or *defaultists*, who take their lead from **Reid**. These commentators – among them **Coady** – argue that there is a default epistemic status enjoyed by testimony-based beliefs such that, in the absence of countervailing considerations, one may legitimately and justifiably form a belief solely on the basis of an instance of testimony. The problem with this approach is that while it is able to avoid the sceptical problems associated with reductionism, it seems to offer little more than a recipe for gullibility. Finding a plausible mid-ground between these two positions has not, however, proved easy. **DHP**

See **credulity, principle of**
Further reading: Coady 1992; Lackey 2005

Theory: In everyday usage, the term 'theory' tends to be employed merely to pick out an integrated set of claims which is being used to explain some general phenomena (as when one says that one has a 'theory' about why the incumbent lost the last election). In the philosophy of science, in contrast, the term tends to be reserved for a set of claims which is being used to make predictions about as yet unobserved events, and which also makes reference to unobserved (and possibly even unobserv*able*) entities. **DHP**

See **observation/theory distinction**
Further reading: Quine 1981

Tracking: The term 'tracking' is often used as a synonym for the **sensitivity** principle, in that to say that a **belief** tracks the **truth** is to say that in the nearest possible world in which what is believed is false, the agent does not believe it (or at least, does not believe it on the same basis as in the actual world). Sometimes, however, tracking is used in a more general way to capture the modal dimension to **knowledge** – the sense in which to know is to have a belief that is suitably sensitive to the relevant facts across a range of defined possible worlds. **DHP**

See **modal epistemology; safety; sensitivity**
Further reading: Nozick 1981

Transcendental arguments: Transcendental arguments are most commonly put forward in response to radical **scepticism**. What exactly is a transcendental argument is a difficult question. The crux of such arguments, however, is to point out that *a* is a necessary condition for the obtaining of *b*, so that *b* cannot obtain without *a*'s obtaining as well. Applied to scepticism, then, a transcendental argument first points out something the sceptic accepts and, second, continues to show that what the sceptic accepts cannot occur *without* knowledge of the external world occurring as well, which makes the sceptical position incoherent. The most famous critic of transcendental arguments is probably Stroud. **MB**

See **scepticism; Strawson, Peter**
Further reading: Stroud 1968

Transcendental idealism: see **idealism; Kant, Immanuel**

Transparency of knowledge: **Knowledge** is a transparent state when, if we know a particular **proposition,** we (are in a position to) know that we know this proposition. This view has been argued against by **Williamson.** According to Williamson, knowledge is not a transparent state. He argues that there are many cases in which a subject knows a proposition but is not in a position to know whether she does. **MB**

See **higher-order knowledge; introspection; iterativity, principle of**
Further reading: Williamson 2000

Tripartite definition of knowledge: One of the core questions in **epistemology** is the question what the nature of **knowledge** is. The standard answer to this question has for long been that knowledge equals justified true **belief.** In order for a subject to know a **proposition,** the subject must truly believe the proposition and must be justified in believing the proposition. This so-called tripartite definition of knowledge has been challenged most famously by **Gettier cases**. Nowadays, almost everyone accepts that the tripartite definition of knowledge isn't adequate: either justification isn't necessary for knowledge after all, or a fourth condition must be added to the tripartite definition of knowledge in order to avoid Gettier **counterexamples**. MB

See **Gettier cases; knowledge; counterexamples**

Further reading: Gettier 1963; Klein 1971

Truth: Since truth is an essential component in **knowledge**, the **theory** of truth has been central to epistemological theorising. Traditionally, theories of truth have fallen into three main camps. First there are the *realist* theories of truth which view truth in terms of some sort of correspondence to the facts. In contrast to realist theories there are *anti-realist* theories that understand truth in epistemic or pragmatic terms as being nothing more than, say, ideal **justification**. Relativistic theories which regard truth as relative in some substantial way, usually to a social milieu, will tend to fall into this category, as will **coherentist** theories of truth. Part of the attraction of anti-realist accounts is the difficulty of specifying the notion of correspondence employed by the realist. Nevertheless, such views have problems of their own, such as an inability to account for our intuition that no matter how well justified a statement is (or how much it coheres with the relevant set of beliefs/propositions), it is still possible for that statement to be false. Finally, there are the *minimalist* or *deflationary* theories which avoid the **realism/anti-realism** debate about truth by contending that truth is not a philosophically important notion at all (in contrast to, say, knowledge). In the extremal case, these views are that there is no difference between asserting a certain sentence and asserting that this sentence is true. This austere version of the deflationary theory of truth is known as the *redundancy* theory, in that it holds that the truth predicate is redundant. Most deflationists do not opt for such an extreme view, however, arguing instead that while the truth predicate is grammatically indispensable, its indispensability does not reflect any central philosophical importance it might have. **DHP**

See **pragmatism; realism/anti-realism; relativism**
Further reading: Engel 2002; Kirkham 1995

Underdetermination: There are two sorts of underdetermination principle in play in the epistemological debate. The first concerns the underdetermination of **theory** relative to **evidence**. This is the thesis – most often associated with the work of **Quine** – that one's choice of theory is always underdetermined by one's evidence, in the sense that there will always be more than one theory that is logically compatible with one's evidence. If this is right, then it seems to imply that theory choice cannot be a matter decided on purely evidential grounds, and thus might not be an epistemic matter at all, strictly speaking.

The second type of underdetermination principle is related to the first, but has more general sceptical implications. This principle – a version of which can plausibly be found in the ancient writings of proponents of **Pyrrhonian scepticism** – maintains that it is a necessary condition of possessing a **justification** for one's **belief** that the evidence one has for one's belief favours the **proposition** believed over all incompatible alternatives (or, at least, all known to be incompatible alternatives). The problem, however, is that it is a key component of the sceptical argument that we are unable to possess evidence which favours our everyday beliefs, such as that I am presently sitting at my desk, over sceptical alternatives, such as the sceptical hypothesis that I am presently a **brain in a vat** being 'fed' experiences as if I am sitting at my desk. A good deal of the focus of the recent discussion on this form of the underdetermination principle has been regarding its relationship to the **closure principle**. Relatedly, the issue of how underdetermination-based **scepticism** and closure-based scepticism are connected to one another, if at all, has also been examined. **DHP**

See **Pyrrhonian scepticism; scepticism**

Further reading: Brueckner 1994; Cohen 1998a; Pritchard 2005b; Quine 1981; Vogel 2004

Understanding: Whereas there has been quite some attention for the notion of understanding in the philosophy of science, 'understanding' is a relatively new topic in **epistemology**. Intuitively, to understand something means to see how things hang together. Or to paraphrase Kvanvig, to understand something means that the subject possesses both a particular body of **information** and can grasp the explanatory connections with respect to that body of information (Kvanvig 2003). The notion of understanding has been discussed particularly in relation to questions about **epistemic value** (for example, questions about what makes knowledge more valuable than mere true belief), where some argue that even if **knowledge** does not possess some sort of intrinsic value, understanding does. **MB**

See **Plato; value, epistemic; wisdom**

Further reading: Kvanvig 2003

Unger, Peter (1942–): An American philosopher, most noted in **epistemology** for his writings on **scepticism** and

infallibilism. Unger's early work is characterised by two key claims. The first is that we should understand **knowledge** in terms of non-lucky, or non-accidental, true **belief.** The second is that 'knowledge' is an **absolute term** in the sense that it describes a property which demands an absolute (and in this case unattainable) standard. More specifically, Unger claims that knowledge entails **certainty** and that 'certainty' is an absolute term since we are only, strictly speaking, properly certain when the target belief is infallible. But since very few, if any, of our beliefs is infallible, it follows that we are rarely properly certain of anything and hence rarely know anything. Unger is therefore able to motivate an **infallibilism**-based scepticism.

In his later work Unger has argued for a weaker thesis whereby the linguistic data is ambivalent between offering support for infallibilism and offering support for **contextualism,** where the latter thesis allows that different epistemic standards can be applicable in different contexts (such that we are sometimes permitted to ascribe knowledge even in the absence of complete infallibility on the part of the agent). Unger argues that such ambivalence is still helpful to the sceptic, however, in that it supports a second-order sceptical **doubt** which holds that we have no good reason not to be sceptics. **DHP**

See **absolute term; certainty; contextualism; ignorance; infallibilism; infallibility; luck, epistemic**

Further reading: Unger 1975; 1984

Value, epistemic: The issue of epistemic value primarily concerns the value of **knowledge** and true **belief.** It might seem obvious that true belief is valuable because of the usefulness of having true beliefs. The problem is that even this instrumental value can be lacking in certain cases, as when one has a true belief in an entirely pointless matter (such as regarding the number of grains of sand on a beach), or when one has a true belief that actually impedes the fulfilment of one's goals (as when one's awareness of the true extent of the danger involved in a situation paralyses one with fear, thereby preventing one from evading the danger in question). These problems transfer to the issue of the value of knowledge. Since it isn't even clear that true belief is always valuable, one cannot simply explain the value of knowledge in terms of the value of this component part of knowledge. Moreover, knowledge too can be of pointless or counterproductive propositions. Nevertheless, it does seem more plausible to suppose that knowledge has at least a greater instrumental value than true belief, and also that all knowledge has some (perhaps limited) intrinsic value – that is, a value that is not dependent upon what use this knowledge can be put to. As Aristotle famously remarked, 'All men by their nature desire to know'. Similarly, it has been argued that even if knowledge in general doesn't possess an intrinsic value, certain kinds of knowledge, like **wisdom** or **understanding**, do.

In recent debate the discussion of epistemic value has tended to focus on whether certain theories of knowledge are in principle unable to account for the value of knowledge over true belief. **Zagzebski** has argued, for example, that externalist theories of knowledge, such as **reliabilism**, are unable to account for the value of knowledge because reliability cannot add value to a true belief. As she puts it, a cup of coffee from a reliable coffee machine is no more valuable because it came from this source than an exactly alike cup of coffee that came from an unreliable machine. In contrast, Zagzebski argues that a **virtue epistemology** understood along the lines that she has developed *can* account for the additional value of knowledge. **DHP**

See **Zagzebski, Linda**

Further reading: Kvanvig 2003; Zagzebski 2003

Verificationism: Verificationism is a radical form of **empiricism** which demands that a statement or thought is only meaningful or intelligible if it is verifiable. If verificationism is accepted then a wide class of statements about matters of fact become problematic, such as many religious, metaphysical, ethical and aesthetical statements. Indeed, ironically, the very statement of the verificationist position would be itself problematic by verificationist lights, since there seems to be no obvious way of verifying it. **DHP**

See **empiricism**

Further reading: Ayer 1946

Virtues: see **intellectual virtues**

Virtue epistemology: A virtue epistemology is any **epistemology** that primarily understands **knowledge** in terms of the **cognitive faculties** and **intellectual virtues**. Early formulations of virtue epistemology – as found in the work of **Sosa** and Greco – were essentially refinements of **reliabilism** (indeed, this early view is often known as agent reliabilism). Whereas a bare process reliabilism faces the problem that there might be processes that are reliable but which have nothing to do with the cognitive character of the agent, and which are thus intuitively not knowledge-supporting at all, these early formulations of virtue epistemology restricted the range of processes relevant to knowledge acquisition to those that were stable parts of an agent's cognitive character, such as the agent's faculties and virtues. So construed, this formulation of virtue epistemology tended to share with reliabilism a commitment to epistemological **externalism**. A related position in this respect is **proper functionalism**, as defended by **Plantinga**, since this also primarily understands knowledge in terms of the reliable functioning of the agent's cognitive traits.

Later versions of virtue epistemology moved away from the reliabilist model by putting more stress on the importance of reflective intellectual virtues to knowledge acquisition, as opposed to the proper functioning of mere cognitive faculties which might demand no reflective capacities on the part of the agent at all. In doing so, these variants of the thesis moved towards epistemically internalist accounts of knowledge which emphasise the agent's responsibility for her beliefs. The foremost proponent of this sort of view is **Zagzebski,** who describes her position as 'neo-Aristotelian'. **DHP**

See **cognitive faculties; intellectual virtues; proper functionalism; reliabilism**

Further reading: Axtell 1997; Greco 1999; Plantinga 1993b; Sosa 1991; Zagzebski 1996

Warrant: The notion 'warrant' can be used to refer to either one of two things. First, it can be used to refer to that which bridges the gap between mere true **belief** and **knowledge**. Here, 'warrant' simply is a placeholder term. Second, it can be used to refer to the specific interpretation put forward by **Plantinga** of that which bridges the gap between mere true belief and knowledge. On Plantinga's view, a belief is warranted if and only if (1) the belief is produced by **cognitive faculties** that are working properly, (2) the segment of the design plan governing the production of the belief is aimed at the production of true beliefs, and (3) there is a high statistical probability that a belief produced under those conditions will be true (Plantinga 1993b). This theory of warrant is heavily externalist (we do not need to know that a belief that p has warrant in order to know a proposition) and is related to reliabilist and virtue-theoretic accounts of knowledge. **MB**

See **cognitive faculties; externalism; Plantinga, Alvin; proper functionalism; reliabilism; virtue epistemology**

Further reading: Kvanvig 1996; Plantinga 1993a, 1993b

Williams, Michael (1947–): A British philosopher, though one who has spent much of his career in the USA. Williams is most noted in **epistemology** for his defence of a form of **contextualism** from which he draws a novel response to the problem of **scepticism**. Williams argues that scepticism is a by-product of what he calls 'epistemological realism', which is **realism** about the objects of epistemological enquiry. Williams argues that this form of realism takes it as given that there is a general structure to **knowledge** which holds across all contexts, an assumption which Williams claims is false. In its place, Williams argues for a radical contextualist thesis – what he refers to as an **epistemic deflationism** – such that in different contexts there are different inferential structures in play governing what may be inferred relative to what, and also different unquestioned assumptions, what Williams calls 'methodological necessities'. This epistemological thesis is meant to be broadly along the lines of the view sketched by **Wittgenstein** in his final notebooks, and the concept of a methodological necessity is very similar to Wittgenstein's own notion of a **hinge proposition**. **DHP**

See **contextualism; deflationism, epistemic; scepticism**
Further reading: Williams 1977, 1991, 2001

Williamson, Timothy (1955–): A British philosopher, whose early career focus was on the philosophy of vagueness and associated disputes in philosophical logic and elsewhere. He advocates an epistemic response to the problem that lays the blame for vagueness on our **ignorance** rather than making vagueness part of the essential fabric of the world. In doing so, Williamson is able to offer a position which is consistent with **realism**. Williamson's recent work has been more explicitly epistemological. He has argued for what he calls a 'knowledge first' approach to **epistemology** which treats **knowledge** as a *sui generis* and indefinable property. In a radical departure from contemporary epistemological theorising, Williamson argues that we should define epistemic and epistemic-related terms like **justification** and **belief** in terms of a primitive conception of knowledge, rather than vice versa.

There are several inter-related features of Williamson's epistemology that are worthy of note. The first is the central place he accords to knowledge in the **explanation** of action. Williamson contends that one cannot adequately explain a whole range of actions without making essential reference to knowledge. Second, Williamson argues for a conception of knowledge that satisfies what he calls a 'margin for error principle'. Very roughly, this principle demands that insofar as one knows a **proposition** then there cannot be a circumstance which most closely resembles the actual circumstances in which the proposition believed is false. Third, Williamson maintains that are no 'luminous' states – that is, states in which in virtue of being in them one knows that one is in them (he refers to this conclusion as 'cognitive homelessness'). Fourth, Williamson offers an account of **assertion** which holds that one should only assert what one knows. Finally, Williamson argues against a phenomenal conception of **evidence,** claiming instead that one's evidence is what one knows. This last claim has radical implications, not least for the problem of **scepticism**. One of the key moves that the sceptic makes is to contend that our evidence in sceptical scenarios in which a sceptical hypothesis is true could well be the same as the evidence we have in non-sceptical scenarios. As Williamson points out, however, this conception of evidence is problematic and, without it, the sceptic is in serious trouble. **DHP**

See **assertion; evidence; luminosity; scepticism**

Further reading: Williamson 1996a, 1996b, 1996c, 2000

Wisdom: There is a tendency in contemporary **epistemology** to shy away from traditional discussions about the nature of **knowledge** and the solution to the Gettier problem, and to focus instead on such forgotten epistemic notions as **understanding** and wisdom. This focus is especially motivated by interest in questions concerning the value of **knowledge**, and interest in questions concerning the epistemic virtues, with some arguing that understanding and wisdom may have some sort of intrinsic value that knowledge itself might be lacking. Indeed, wisdom is often thought of as the highest epistemic good attainable. **MB**

See **intellectual virtues; understanding; value, epistemic; virtue epistemology**

Further reading: Riggs 2003

Wishful thinking: Most epistemologists agree that **knowledge** must be analysed in terms of true **belief** and also agree that true belief by itself isn't sufficient for knowledge. So the pivotal question is: what must be added to true belief to yield knowledge? There is stark disagreement over the correct answer to this question, though most epistemologists implicitly endorse that the third condition for knowledge must be an anti-luck condition: in order to know, it must not be the case that one luckily truly believes a proposition. Hence, wishful thinking, though a source of belief (and in some cases even a source of true belief), is ruled out as a source of non-lucky true belief, and, thus, knowledge. **MB**

See **luck, epistemic; reliabilism; warrant**

Further reading: Goldman 1979; Pritchard 2005a

Wittgenstein, Ludwig (1889–1951): An Austrian philosopher, though one who spent most of his academic career at Cambridge University, Wittgenstein has been perhaps the most influential philosopher of the last 100 years. His importance to **epistemology** mainly concerns two areas of his work. The first is his remarks on **knowledge** and **certainty** that are found in his final notebooks (published as *On Certainty*). Here Wittgenstein argues for a radical picture of the structure of **reasons** which highlights the ultimately groundless nature of **belief**. Instead of grounds of a special sort underpinning our beliefs, Wittgenstein argues that what we find instead is simply a shared set of beliefs about which we are completely certain – what he referred to as '**hinge propositions**'. His work in the philosophy of mind, and his related remarks on **the problem of rule-following**, also have important epistemological ramifications. Wittgenstein argued, for example, for a conception of the relationship between pain and pain behaviour which makes use of the notion of **criteria** and which lays a great deal of stress on the epistemological importance of **avowals** in this regard. Wittgenstein also attacked the idea of a private language which he believed to be implicit in much of the thinking about the mind at the time. Rather than conceiving of language acquisition as being in terms of a mapping of already established private meanings onto public meanings, Wittgenstein instead emphasised the essentially *social* aspect of language acquisition. In doing so he also raised important questions about what it means to follow a rule. **DHP**

See **avowals; criteria; hinge propositions; private language argument; rule-following, problem of**

Further reading: Pears 1987–8; Wittgenstein 1953, 1969

Wright, Crispin (1942–): A British philosopher, Wright is most known for his development of a brand of **anti-realism** which draws upon earlier work by **Dummett**. In his more recent writings he has begun to engage with such epistemological questions as the nature of **question-begging arguments**, the putative consistency of **content externalism** and **first-person authority**, and the problem of **scepticism**. Indeed, Wright thinks that there is a common resolution to all these issues, with the key lying in the Wittgensteinian notion of a hinge proposition, a proposition which, Wright argues, we are epistemically entitled to believe even whilst lacking a **warrant** to believe. **DHP**

See **anti-realism; hinge propositions; truth**

Further reading: Wright 1985, 1991a, 1991b, 1992, 1993, 2000, 2003, 2004

Zagzebski, Linda (1946–): American philosopher, most noted in **epistemology** for her development of a neo-Aristotelian **virtue epistemology**. Like all virtue epistemologies, this view essentially understands **knowledge** in terms of reliable belief-forming traits. What is distinctive about Zagzebski's position, however, is that she also insists on a motivational component to her view. In so doing, she ensures that knowledge could not merely come about as the result of a reliable cognitive faculty, but requires also the sort of broadly reflective capacities involved in the exercise of an intellectual virtue. This is in contrast to the main body of virtue epistemologies, which are essentially refined versions of **reliabilism**. Zagzebski's goal is to offer a philosophical position which can integrate a virtue epistemology with a virtue ethic and thereby present us with a unified theory of the good life that deals with both ethical and epistemological aspects. It is only by offering a theory of this sort, argues Zagzebski, that one can account for the value of knowledge. **DHP**

See **intellectual virtue; value, epistemic; virtue epistemology**

Further reading: Zagzebski 1996

Bibliography

Achinstein, P. (1983), *The Nature of Explanation*, Oxford: Oxford University Press.

Alcoff, L. and Potter, E. (eds) (1993), *Feminist Epistemologies*, New York: Routledge.

Almeida, C. de (2001), 'What Moore's Paradox is About', *Philosophy and Phenomenological Research* 62, 33–58.

Alston, W. P. (1980), 'Level Confusion in Epistemology', *Midwest Studies in Philosophy* 5, 135–50.

Alston, W. P. (1983), 'What's Wrong with Immediate Knowledge?', *Synthese* 55, 73–95.

Alston, W. P. (1986), 'Internalism and Externalism in Epistemology', *Philosophical Topics* 14, 179–221.

Alston, W. P. (1989), *Epistemic Justification*, Ithaca, NY: Cornell University Press.

Alston, W. P. (1991), *Perceiving God: The Epistemology of Religious Experience*, Ithaca, NY: Cornell University Press.

Alston, W. P. (1993a), 'Epistemic Desiderata', *Philosophy and Phenomenological Research* 53, 527–51.

Alston, W. P. (1993b), *The Reliability of Sense Perception*, Ithaca, NY: Cornell University Press.

Alston, W. P. (1995), 'How to Think about Reliability', *Philosophical Topics* 23, 1–29.

Alston, W. P. (1999), 'Perceptual Knowledge', in J. Greco (ed.), *The Blackwell Guide to Epistemology*, Oxford: Blackwell Publishers, 223–43.

Alston, W. P. (2005), *Beyond Justification: Dimensions of Epistemic Evaluation*, Ithaca, NY: Cornell University Press.

Annis, D. (1978), 'A Contextualist Theory of Epistemic Justification', *American Philosophical Quarterly* 15, 213–19.

Armstrong, D. M. (1963), 'Is Introspective Knowledge Incorrigible?', *Philosophical Topics* 21, 1–20.

Armstrong, D. M. (1973), *Belief, Truth and Knowledge*, Cambridge: Cambridge University Press.

Atherton, M. (ed.) (1999), *The Empiricists: Critical Essays on Locke, Berkeley, and Hume*, Totowa, NJ: Rowman and Littlefield.

Austin, J. L. (1961a), 'Other Minds', in Austin (1961b); also *Proceedings of the Aristotelian Society* (1946), 20: 148–87.

Austin, J. L. (1961b), *Philosophical Papers*, Oxford: Oxford University Press.

Austin, J. L. (1962a), *Sense and Sensibilia*, Oxford: Oxford University Press.

Austin, J. L. (1962b), *How To Do Things With Words*, Oxford: Oxford University Press.

Axtell, G. (1997), 'Recent Work on Virtue Epistemology', *American Philosophical Quarterly* 34, 1–26.

Ayer, A. J. (1946), *Language, Truth and Logic*, London: Gollancz.

Ayer, A. J. (1947), *The Foundations of Empirical Knowledge*, London: Macmillan.

Ayer, A. J. (1956), *The Problem of Knowledge*, London: Macmillan.

Bird, G. (1987), *William James*, London: Routledge and Kegan Paul.

Bergmann, M. (1997), 'Internalism, Externalism, and the No-Defeater Condition', *Synthese* 110, 399–417.

Blaauw, M. (2004), *Contrastivism: Reconciling Sceptical Doubt with Ordinary Knowledge*, PhD dissertation, Vrije Universiteit Amsterdam.

Black, T. (2003), 'The Relevant Alternatives Theory and Missed Clues', *Australasian Journal of Philosophy* 81, 96–106.

Bodgan, R. (ed.) (1987), *Jaakko Hintikka*, Dordrecht: Kluwer.

BonJour, L. (1978), 'A Critique of Foundationalism', *American Philosophical Quarterly* 15, 1–13.

BonJour, L. (1985), *The Structure of Empirical Knowledge*, Cambridge, MA: Harvard University Press.

BonJour, L. (1998), *In Defence of Pure Reason*, Cambridge: Cambridge University Press.

BonJour, L. (2002), *Epistemology: Classic Problems and Contemporary Responses*, Lanham, MD: Rowman and Littlefield.

BonJour, L. and Sosa, E. (2003), *Epistemic Justification: Internalism vs Externalism, Foundationalism vs Virtues*, Oxford: Blackwell Publishers.

Bovens, L. and Hartmann, S. (2004), *Bayesian Epistemology*, Oxford: Oxford University Press.

Brady, M. and Pritchard, D. H. (eds) (2003), *Moral and Epistemic Virtues*, Oxford: Blackwell.

Brock, S. and Mares, E. (2005), *Realism and Anti-realism*, Chesham: Acumen Press.

Brueckner, A. (1994), 'The Structure of the Skeptical Argument', *Philosophy and Phenomenological Research* 54, 827–35.

Brueckner, A. (2003), 'What Missed Clue Cases Show', *Analysis* 63, 303–5.

Campbell, D. T. (1974), 'Evolutionary Epistemology', in P. A. Schilpp (ed.), *The Philosophy of Karl R. Popper*, LaSalle, IL: Open Court, 412–63.

Campbell, J. (1995), *Understanding John Dewey*, Chicago, IL: Open Court.

Casullo, A. (2003), *A Priori Justification*, New York: Oxford University Press.

Chappell, V. (1994), *The Cambridge Companion to John Locke*, Cambridge: Cambridge University Press.

Chisholm, R. M. (1957), *Perceiving: A Philosophical Study*, Ithaca, NY: Cornell University Press.

Chisholm, R. M. (1973), *The Problem of the Criterion*, Milwaukee, WI: Marquette University Press

Chisholm, R. M. (1988), 'The Indispensability of Internal Justification', *Synthese* 74, 285–96.

Chisholm, R. M. (1982a), 'Knowing That One Knows', in Chisholm (1982b), ch. 3.

Chisholm, R. M. (1982b), *The Foundations of Knowing*, Minneapolis, MN: University of Minnesota Press.

Chisholm, R. M. (1989), *Theory of Knowledge* (3rd edn), Englewood Cliffs, NJ: Prentice Hall.

Clark, P. and Hale, B. (eds) (1995), *Reading Putnam*, Oxford: Blackwell.

Coady, C. A. J. (1992), *Testimony: A Philosophical Study*, Oxford: Clarendon Press.

Coates, P. (2005), *Metaphysics of Perception: Wilfrid Sellars, Critical Realism, and the Nature of Experience*, London: Routledge.

Cohen, L. J. (1992), *An Essay on Belief and Acceptance*, Oxford: Oxford University Press.

Cohen, S. (1991), 'Skepticism, Relevance, and Relativity', in McLaughlin (1991), 17–37.

Cohen, S. (1998a), 'Two Kinds of Skeptical Argument', *Philosophy and Phenomenological Research* 58, 143–59.

Cohen, S. (1998b), 'Contextualist Solution to Epistemological Problems: Scepticism, Gettier, and the Lottery', *Australasian Journal of Philosophy* 76, 289–306.

Cohen, S. (2000), 'Contextualism and Skepticism', *Philosophical Issues* 10, 94–107.

Conee, E. and Feldman, R. (1985), 'Evidentialism', *Philosophical Studies* 48, 15–34.

Conee, E. and Feldman, R. (1998), 'The Generality Problem for Reliabilism', *Philosophical Studies* 89, 1–29.

Conee, E. and Feldman, R. (2001), 'Internalism Defended', in Kornblith, H. (2001), 231–61.

Conee, E. and Feldman, R. (2004), *Evidentialism: Essays in Epistemology*, New York: Oxford University Press.

Cottingham, J. (1992), *The Cambridge Companion to Descartes*, Cambridge: Cambridge University Press.

Cuneo, T. and van Woudenberg, R. (eds) (2004), *The Cambridge Companion to Thomas Reid*, Cambridge: Cambridge University Press.

Dancy, J. (1987), *Berkeley: An Introduction*, Oxford: Blackwell.

Dancy, J. (1993), *Moral Reasons*, Oxford: Blackwell.

Davidson, D. (1986), 'A Coherence Theory of Truth and Knowledge', in E. LePore (ed.) (1986), ch. 16.

Davidson, D. (2001a), *Inquiries into Truth and Interpretation*, Oxford: Oxford University Press.

Davidson, D. (2001b), *Subjective, Intersubjective, Objective*, Oxford: Oxford University Press.

Davidson, D. (2004), *Problems of Rationality: Philosophical Essays*, Oxford: Oxford University Press.

DeRose, K. (1995), 'Solving the Skeptical Problem', *Philosophical Review* 104, 1–52.

DeRose, K. (2002), 'Knowledge, Assertion, and Context', *Philosophical Review* 111, 167–203.

Descartes, R. (1975), *The Philosophical Writings of Descartes*, ed. J. Cottingham, R. Stoothoff, and D. Murdoch, Cambridge: Cambridge University Press.

Dewey, J. (1969–90), *The Early Works of John Dewey, 1882–1898; The Middle Works of John Dewey, 1899–1924; The Later Works of John Dewey, 1925–1953* (37 vols), ed. J. A. Boydston, Carbondale, IL: Southern Illinois Press.

Dretske, F. (1969), *Seeing and Knowing*, London: Routledge and Kegan Paul.

Dretske, F. (1970), 'Epistemic Operators', *The Journal of Philosophy* 67, 1007–23.

Dretske, F. (1971), 'Conclusive Reasons', *Australasian Journal of Philosophy* 49, 1–22.

Dretske, F. (1981), *Knowledge and the Flow of Information*, Oxford: Blackwell.

Dretske, F. (1995), *Naturalizing the Mind*, Cambridge, MA: MIT Press.

Dretske, F. (2000), *Perception, Knowledge and Belief*, Cambridge: Cambridge University Press.

Dummett, M. (1978), *Truth and other Enigmas*, Cambridge, MA: Harvard University Press.

Engel, P. (2002), *Truth*, Chesham: Acumen Press.

Feldman, R. (1985), 'Reliability and Justification', *The Monist* 68, 159–74.

Feldman, R. (1988), 'Epistemic Obligations', *Philosophical Perspectives* 2, 235–56.

Fogelin, R. (1980), *Wittgenstein*, London: Routledge.

Fogelin, R. (1994), *Pyrrhonian Reflections on Knowledge and Justification*, Oxford: Oxford University Press.

Fogelin, R. (2001), *Berkeley and the 'Principles of Human Knowledge'*, London: Routledge.

Fogelin, R. (2003), *A Defense of Hume on Miracles*, Princeton, NJ: Princeton University Press.

Fogelin, R. and Sinnott-Armstrong, W. (2001), *Understanding Arguments: An Introduction to Informal Logic*, San Diego, CA: Harcourt College Publishers.

Foley, R. (1987), *A Theory of Epistemic Rationality*, Cambridge, MA: Harvard University Press.

Foley, R. (1993), *Working Without a Net*, Oxford: Oxford University Press.

Foley, R. (forthcoming), 'What must be Added to True Beliefs in order to have Knowledge? Answer: More True Beliefs', *Philosophy and Phenomenological Research* 67.

Foster, J. (1985), *A. J. Ayer*, London: Routledge and Kegan Paul.

Fraassen, B. Van (1980), *The Scientific Image*, Oxford: Oxford University Press.

Gallois, A. (1996), *The World Without, the Mind Within: An Essay on First-Person Authority*, Cambridge: Cambridge University Press.

Garrett, D. (ed.) (1997), *Encyclopaedia of Empiricism*, Westport, CT: Greenwood Press.

Gendler, T. (2000), 'The Puzzle of Imaginative Resistance', *The Journal of Philosophy*, XCVII: 2, 55–81.

Gendler, T. and Hawthorne, J. (2002), *Conceivability and Possibility*, Oxford: Oxford University Press.

Gendler, T. and Hawthorne, J. (forthcoming), 'The Real Guide to Fake Barns', *Philosophical Studies*.

Gettier, E. (1963), 'Is Justified True Belief Knowledge?', *Analysis* 23, 121–3.

Goldman, A. (1967), 'A Causal Theory of Knowing', *The Journal of Philosophy* 64, 355–72.

Goldman, A. (1976), 'Discrimination and Perceptual Knowledge', *The Journal of Philosophy* 73, 771–91.

Goldman, A. (1979), 'What is Justified Belief?', in G. S. Pappas (ed.), *Justification and Knowledge*, Dordrecht: Reidel, 1–23.

Goldman, A. (1986), *Epistemology and Cognition*, Cambridge, MA: Harvard University Press.

Goldman, A. (1992), *Liaisons: Philosophy Meets the Cognitive and Social Sciences*, Cambridge, MA: MIT Press.

Goldman, A. (1999), *Knowledge in a Social World*, Oxford: Oxford University Press.

Goldman, A. (2001), 'Experts: Which Ones Should You Trust?', in Goldman (2002), 139–63.

Goldman, A. (2002), *Pathways to Knowledge: Private and Public*, Oxford: Oxford University Press.

Goodman, N, (1965), *Fact, Fiction and Forecast*, Indianapolis, IN: Bobbs Merrill.

Greco, J. (1999), 'Agent Reliabilism', *Philosophical Perspectives* 13, 273–96.

Greco, J. (2000), *Putting Sceptics in their Place*, Cambridge: Cambridge University Press.

Greco, J. (ed.) (2004), *Ernest Sosa and His Critics*, Oxford: Blackwell.

Grice, H. P. (1989), *Studies in the Way of Words*, Cambridge, MA: Harvard University Press.

Haack, S. (1993), *Evidence and Inquiry: Towards Reconstruction in Epistemology*, Oxford: Blackwell.

Habermas, J. (1971), *Knowledge and Human Interests*, Heinemann: London.

Habermas, J. (1984–7), *The Theory of Communicative Action* (2 vols), Cambridge: Polity.

Hahn, L. E. (ed.) (1998), *The Philosophy of P. F. Strawson*, Chicago, IL: Open Court.

Harre, R. and Krausz, M. (eds) (1995), *Varieties of Relativism*, Oxford: Blackwell.

Haslanger, S. (ed.) (1995), *Feminist Perspectives on Language, Knowledge and Reality*, special issue of *Philosophical Topics*.

Hawthorne, J. (2004), *Knowledge and Lotteries*, Oxford: Clarendon Press.

Heck, R. (1998), *Logic, Language, and Reality: Essays in Honour of Michael Dummett*, Oxford: Oxford University Press.

Heil, J. (1983), 'Doxastic Agency', *Philosophical Studies* 40, 355–64.

Helm, P. (1994), *Belief Policies*, Cambridge: Cambridge University Press.

Hempel, C. G. (1965), *Aspects of Scientific Explanation*, New York: The Free Press.

Hintikka, J. (1962), *Knowledge and Belief: An Introduction to the Logic of the Two Notions*, Ithaca, NY: Cornell University Press.

Hintikka, J. (1974), *Knowledge and the Known: Historical Perspectives in Epistemology*, Dordrecht: Reidel.

Holland, J. H., Holyoak, K. J., Nisbett, R. E. and Thagard, P. R. (1989), *Induction: Processes of Inference, Learning and Discovery*, Cambridge, MA: MIT Press.

Hookway, C. (1985), *Peirce*, London: Routledge and Kegan Paul.

Hookway, C. (1988), *Quine: Language, Experience and Reality*, Stanford, CA: Stanford University Press.

Houston, J. (1994), *Reported Miracles*, Cambridge: Cambridge University Press.

Hume, D. (1989) [1777], *Enquiries Concerning Human Understanding and Concerning the Principles of Morals*, ed. P. Nidditch, Oxford: Clarendon Press.

Jackson, F. (1998), *From Metaphysics to Ethics*, Oxford: Clarendon Press.

James, W. (1961), *The Varieties of Religious Experience*, London: Macmillan.

James, W. (1975a), *Pragmatism: A New Name for Some Old Ways of Thinking*, Cambridge, MA: Harvard University Press.

James, W. (1975b), *The Meaning of Truth: A Sequel to Pragmatism*, Cambridge, MA: Harvard University Press.

James, W. (1976), *Essays in Radical Empiricism*, Cambridge, MA: Harvard University Press.

Kant, I. (1998) [1781], *The Critique of Pure Reason*, trans. P. Guyer and A. W. Wood, Cambridge: Cambridge University Press.

Kirk, R. (1999), *Relativism and Reality: A Contemporary Introduction*, London: Routledge.

Kirkham, R. (1995), *Theories of Truth: A Critical Introduction*, Cambridge, MA: MIT Press.

Kitcher, P. (1983), *The Nature of Mathematical Knowledge*, New York: Oxford University Press.

Klein, P. (1971), 'A Proposed Definition of Propositional Knowledge', *Journal of Philosophy* 68, 471–82.

Klein, P. (1981), *Certainty: A Refutation of Scepticism*, Minneapolis, MN: University of Minnesota Press.

Klein, P. (1998), 'Foundationalism and the Infinite Regress of Reasons', *Philosophy and Phenomenological Research* 58, 919–25.

Kornblith, H. (ed.) (1985), *Naturalizing Epistemology*, Cambridge, MA: MIT Press.

Kornblith, H. (ed.) (2001), *Epistemology: Internalism and External-ism*, Oxford: Blackwell.

Kornblith, H. (2002), *Knowledge and its Place in Nature*, Oxford: Oxford University Press.

Kornblith, H. (2003), 'Roderick Chisholm and the Shaping of American Epistemology', *Metaphilosophy* 34: 5, 582–602.

Kretzmann, N. and Stump, E. (1993), *The Cambridge Companion to Aquinas*, Cambridge: Cambridge University Press.

Kripke, S. (1982), *Wittgenstein on Rules and Private Language*, Oxford: Blackwell.

Kvanvig, J. (1992), *The Intellectual Virtues and the Life of the Mind: On the Place of the Virtues in Contemporary Epistemology*, Savage, MD: Rowman and Littlefield.

Kvanvig, J. (ed.) (1996), *Warrant in Contemporary Epistemology: Essays in Honour of Alvin Plantinga's Epistemology*, Totowa, NJ: Rowman and Littlefield.

Kvanvig, J. (2003), *The Value of Knowledge and the Pursuit of Understanding*, Cambridge: Cambridge University Press.

Kyburg, H. (1961), *Probability and the Logic of Rational Belief*, Middletown, CT: Wesleyan University Press.

Lackey, J. (ed.) (2005), *The Epistemology of Testimony*, Oxford: Oxford University Press.

Langton, R. (1998), *Kantian Humility. Our Ignorance of Things in Themselves*, Oxford: Oxford University Press.

Lehrer, K. (1974), *Knowledge*, Oxford: Oxford University Press.

Lehrer, K. (1989), *Thomas Reid*, London: Routledge.

Lehrer, K. (1990a), *Metamind*, Oxford: Clarendon Press.

Lehrer, K. (1990b), *Theory of Knowledge*, Boulder, CO: Westview Press.

Lehrer, K. (1997), *Self-trust: A Study of Reason, Knowledge and Autonomy,* Oxford: Clarendon Press.

Lehrer, K. (1999), 'Rationality', in J. Greco (ed.), *The Blackwell Guide to Epistemology*, Oxford: Blackwell, 206–21.

LePore. E. (ed.) (1986), *Truth and Interpretation: Perspectives on the Philosophy of Donald Davidson*, Oxford: Blackwell.

Levy, I. (1980), *The Enterprise of Knowledge*, Cambridge, MA: MIT Press.

Lewis, D. (1979), 'Scorekeeping in a Language Game', *Journal of Philosophical Logic* 8, 339–59.

Lewis, D. (1996), 'Elusive Knowledge', *Australasian Journal of Philosophy* 74, 549–67.

Lipton, P. (1991), *Inference to the Best Explanation*, London: Routledge.

Locke, J. (1979) [1690], *An Essay Concerning Human Understanding*, ed. P. Nidditch, Oxford: Clarendon Press.

Loftus, E. (2003), 'Make-Believe Memories', *American Psychologist* 58, 867–73.

Longino, H. (1990), *Science as Social Knowledge*, Princeton, NJ: Princeton University Press.

Luper-Foy, S. (ed.) (1987), *The Possibility of Knowledge: Nozick and His Critics*, Totowa, NJ: Rowman and Littlefield.

Lyons, W. (1988), *The Disappearance of Introspection*, Cambridge, MA: MIT Press.

Malachowski, A. (2002), *Richard Rorty*, Princeton, NJ: Princeton University Press.

Mavrodes, G. (1970), *Belief in God: A Study in the Epistemology of Religion*, New York: Random House.

Mavrodes, G. (1988), *Revelation in Religious Belief*, Philadelphia, PA: Temple University Press.

McDowell, J. (1994), *Mind and World*, Cambridge, MA: Harvard University Press.

McDowell, J. (2001a), *Meaning, Knowledge and Reality*, Cambridge, MA: Harvard University Press.

McDowell, J. (2001b), *Mind, Value and Reality*, Cambridge, MA: Harvard University Press.

McLaughlin, B. (ed.) (1991), *Dretske and His Critics*, Oxford: Blackwell.

McManus, D. (ed.) (2003), *Wittgenstein and Scepticism*, London: Routledge.

Millar, A. (1991), *Reasons and Experience*, Oxford: Clarendon Press.

Miller, R. W. (1995), 'The Norms of Reason', *Philosophical Review* 104, 205–45.

Moore, G. E. (1925), 'A Defence of Common Sense', in Muirhead 1925, ch. 5.

Moore, G. E. (1939), 'Proof of an External World', *Proceedings of the British Academy* 25, 273–300.

Muirhead, J. H. (ed.) (1925), *Contemporary British philosophy*, 2nd series, London: Allen and Unwin.

Neta, R. (2002), 'Contextualism and the Problem of the External World', *Philosophy and Phenomenological Research* 66, 1–31.

Neta, R. and Rohrbaugh, G. (2004), 'Luminosity and the Safety of Knowledge', *Pacific Philosophical Quarterly* 85, 396–406.

Norton, D. (1993), *The Cambridge Companion to David Hume*, Cambridge: Cambridge University Press.

Nozick, R. (1981), *Philosophical Explanations*, Oxford: Oxford University Press.

Nuccetelli, S. (ed.) (2003), *New Essays on Semantic Externalism and Self-Knowledge*, Cambridge, MA: MIT Press.

O'Hear, A. (1980), *Karl Popper*, London: Routledge and Kegan Paul.

Olsson, E. (2003), *The Epistemology of Keith Lehrer*, Dordrecht: Kluwer.

Paley, W. (1825), *The Works of William Paley, D. D. Archdeacon of Carlisle*, Edinburgh: Peter Brown and T. W. Nelson.

Pears, D. F. (1987–8), *The False Prison* (2 vols), Oxford: Oxford University Press.

Peirce, C. S. (1931–58), *Collected Papers of Charles S. Peirce* (8 vols), Cambridge, MA: Harvard University Press.

Plantinga, A. (1967), *God and Other Minds*, Ithaca, NY: Cornell University Press.

Plantinga, A. (1974), *The Nature of Necessity*, Oxford: Oxford University Press.

Plantinga, A. (1983), 'Reason and Belief in God', in Plantinga, A. and Wolterstorff, N. (eds), *Faith and Rationality*, Notre Dame, IN: Notre Dame University Press.

Plantinga, A. (1993a), *Warrant: The Current Debate*, Oxford: Oxford University Press.

Plantinga, A. (1993b), *Warrant and Proper Function*, Oxford: Oxford University Press.

Plantinga, A. (2000), *Warranted Christian Belief*, Oxford: Oxford University Press.

Plato (1997), *The Dialogues of Plato*, trans. R. E. Allen, New Haven, CT: Yale University Press.

Pollock, J. (1974), *Knowledge and Justification*, Princeton, NJ: Princeton University Press.

Pollock, J. (1986), *Contemporary Theories of Knowledge*, Totowa, NJ: Rowman and Littlefield.

Popper, K. (1959), *The Logic of Scientific Discovery*, London: Hutchinson.

Popper, K. (1963), *Conjectures and Refutations*, London: Routledge and Kegan Paul.

Popper, K. (1972), *Objective Knowledge*, Oxford: Clarendon Press.

Popper, K. (1983), *Realism and the Aim of Science*, London: Hutchinson.

Pritchard, D. H. (2002), 'Resurrecting the Moorean Response to Scepticism', *International Journal of Philosophical Studies* 10, 283–307.

Pritchard, D. H. (2003), 'Reforming Reformed Epistemology', *International Philosophical Quarterly* 43, 43–66.

Pritchard, D. H. (2004), 'Epistemic Deflationism', *The Southern Journal of Philosophy* 42, 1–32.

Pritchard, D. H. (2005a), *Epistemic Luck*, Oxford: Oxford University Press.

Pritchard, D. H. (2005b), 'The Structure of Sceptical Arguments', *The Philosophical Quarterly* 55, 37–52.

Pryor, J. (2000), 'The Sceptic and the Dogmatist', *Nous* 34, 517–49.

Putnam, H. (1981), *Reason, Truth and History*, Cambridge: Cambridge University Press.

Putnam, H. (1983), *Realism and Reason*, Cambridge: Cambridge University Press.

Putnam, H. (1987), *The Many Faces of Realism*, La Salle, PA: Open Court.

Putnam, H. (1989), *Representation and Reality*, Cambridge, MA: MIT Press.

Putnam, H. (1992), *Renewing Philosophy*, Cambridge, MA: Harvard University Press.

Quine, W. V. O. (1960), *Word and Object*, Cambridge, MA: MIT Press.

Quine, W. V. O. (1969a), 'Epistemology Naturalised', in Quine 1969b, 69–90.

Quine, W. V. O. (1969b), *Ontological Relativity and Other Essays*, New York: Columbia University Press.

Quine, W. V. O. (1973), *The Roots of Reference*, La Salle, PA: Open Court.

Quine, W. V. O. (1981), *Theories and Things*, Cambridge, MA: Harvard University Press.

Quine, W. V. O. (1990), *Pursuit of Truth*, Cambridge, MA: Harvard University Press.

Radford, C. (1966), 'Knowledge – by Examples', *Analysis* 27, 1–11.

Reichenbach, H. (1938), *Experience and Prediction: An Analysis of the Foundation and the Structure of Knowledge*, Chicago, IL: University of Chicago Press.

Reichenbach, H. (1949), *Theory of Probability*, Berkeley, CA: University of California Press.

Richards, M. (2004), 'Contextualism and Relativism', *Philosophical Studies* 119, 215–42.

Riggs, W. (2003), 'Understanding Virtue and the Virtue of Understanding', in M. DePaul and L. Zagzebski (eds), *Intellectual Virtue: Perspectives from Ethics and Epistemology*, Oxford: Oxford University Press, 203–27.

Roeser, S. (2002), *Ethical Intuitions and Emotions*, PhD thesis Vrije Universiteit, Amsterdam.

Rorty, R. (1979), *Philosophy and the Mirror of Nature*, Princeton, NJ: Princeton University Press.

Rorty, R. (1982), *Consequences of Pragmatism*, Minneapolis, MN: University of Minnesota Press.

Rorty, R. (1989), *Contingency, Irony and Solidarity*, Cambridge: Cambridge University Press.

Rorty, R. (1991), *Essays on Reality and Representation*, Cambridge: Cambridge University Press.

Rorty, R. (1998), *Truth and Progress*, Cambridge: Cambridge University Press.

Russell, B. (1912), *Problems of Philosophy*, Oxford: Oxford University Press.

Ryle, G. (1949), *The Concept of Mind*, London: Hutchinson.

Salmon, W. (1979), *Hans Reichenbach: Logical Empiricist*, Dordrecht: Kluwer.

Salmon, N. and Soames, S. (eds) (1989), *Propositions and Attitudes*, Oxford: Oxford University Press.

Sartwell, C. (1991), 'Knowledge is Merely True Belief', *American Philosophical Quarterly* 28, 157–65.

Schaffer, J. (2001), 'Knowledge, Relevant Alternatives, and Missed Clues', *Analysis* 61, 202–8.

Schaffer, J. (2004), 'From Contextualism to Contrastivism in Epistemology', *Philosophical Studies* 119, 73–103.

Schaffer, J. (2005a), 'Contrastive Knowledge', in T. Gendler and J. Hawthorne (eds), *Oxford Studies in Epistemology*, Oxford: Oxford University Press.

Schaffer, J. (2005b), 'Skepticism, Contextualism, and Discrimination', *Philosophy and Phenomenological Research* 69, 138–55.

Schaffer, J. (2005c), 'Knowing the Answer', unpublished.

Sellars, W. (1963), *Science, Perception and Reality*, London: Routledge and Kegan Paul.

Sellars, W. (1997), *Empiricism and the Philosophy of Mind*, Cambridge, MA: Harvard University Press.

Sextus Empiricus (1933–49), *Sextus Empiricus with an English Translation* (4 vols), trans. R. G. Bury, London: Heinemann.

Shope, R. K. (1983), *The Analysis of Knowing: A Decade of Research*, Princeton, NJ: Princeton University Press.

Sinnott-Armstrong, W. and Timmons, M. (eds) (1995), *Moral Knowledge? New Readings in Moral Epistemology*, New York: Oxford University Press.

Skorupski, J. (1998), *The Cambridge Companion to John Stuart Mill*, Cambridge: Cambridge University Press.

Smith, N. (ed.) (2002), *Reading McDowell: On Mind and World*, London: Routledge.

Sosa, E. (1980), 'The Raft and the Pyramid', *Midwest Studies in Philosophy* 5, 3–25.

Sosa, E. (1985), 'Knowledge and Intellectual Virtue', *The Monist* 68, 226–45.

Sosa, E. (1986), 'On Knowledge and Context', *The Journal of Philosophy* 83, 584–5.

Sosa, E. (1991), *Knowledge in Perspective: Selected Essays in Epistemology*, Cambridge: Cambridge University Press.

Sosa, E. (1999a), 'How to Defeat Opposition to Moore', *Philosophical Perspectives* 13, 141–54.

Sosa, E. (1999b), 'How Must Knowledge be Modally Related to What is Known?', *Philosophical Topics* 26, 373–84.

Sosa, E. (2003), 'Chisholm's Epistemic Principles', *Metaphilosophy* 34: 5, 553–62.

Stalnaker, R. (2004), 'Comments on "From Contextualism to Contrastivism"', *Philosophical Studies* 119, 105–17.

Stanley, J. and Williamson, T. (2001), 'Knowing How', *Journal of Philosophy* XCVIII, 411–44.

Stine, G. C. (1976), 'Skepticism, Relevant Alternatives, and Deductive Closure', *Philosophical Studies* 29, 249–61.

Strawson, P. F. (1959), *Individuals: An Essay in Descriptive Metaphysics*, London: Methuen.

Strawson, P. F. (1967), *The Bounds of Sense*, London: Methuen.

Strawson, P. F. (1985), *Scepticism and Naturalism*, London: Methuen.

Stroud, B. (1968), 'Transcendental Arguments', *Journal of Philosophy* 65, 241–56.

Stroud, B. (1984), *The Significance of Philosophical Scepticism*, Oxford: Clarendon Press.

Stroud, B. (2002), *The Quest for Reality: Subjectivism and the Metaphysics of Colour*, Oxford: Oxford University Press.

Swinburne, R. (1979), *The Existence of God*, Oxford: Clarendon Press.

Swinburne, R. (1983), *Faith and Reason*, Oxford: Clarendon Press.

Swinburne, R. (1992), *Revelation. From Metaphor to Analogy*, Oxford: Clarendon Press.

Thayer, H. S. (ed.) (1982), *Pragmatism: The Classic Writings*, London: Hackett.

Unger, P. (1968), 'An Analysis of Factual Knowledge', *Journal of Philosophy* 65, 157–70.

Unger, P. (1975), *Ignorance: A Case for Scepticism*, Oxford: Oxford University Press.

Unger, P. (1984), *Philosophical Relativity*, Oxford: Blackwell.

Vogel, J. (1990), 'Cartesian Skepticism and Inference to the Best Explanation', *Journal of Philosophy* 87, 658–66.

Vogel, J. (2004), 'Varieties of Skepticism', *Philosophy and Phenomenological Research* 68, 1–37.

Warnock, G. J. (1980), *J. L. Austin*, London: Routledge and Kegan Paul.

Weatherson, B. (2003), 'What Good are Counterexamples?', *Philosophical Studies* 115, 1–31.

White, S. (ed.) (1995), *The Cambridge Companion to Habermas*, Cambridge: Cambridge University Press.

Williams, M. (1977), *Groundless Belief: An Essay on the Possibility of Knowledge*, Yale, CT: Yale University Press.

Williams, M. (1991), *Unnatural Doubts: Epistemological Realism and the Philosophical Basis of Scepticism*, Princeton, NJ: Princeton University Press.

Williams, M. (2001), *Problems of Knowledge: A Critical Introduction to Epistemology*, Oxford: Oxford University Press.

Williamson, T. (1996a), 'Cognitive Homelessness', *Journal of Philosophy* 93, 554–73.

Williamson, T. (1996b), 'Knowing and Asserting', *Philosophical Review* 105, 489–523.

Williamson, T. (1996c), *Vagueness*, London: Routledge.

Williamson, T. (2000), *Knowledge and its Limits*, Oxford: Oxford University Press.

Wittgenstein, L. (1953), *Philosophical Investigations*, trans. G. E. M. Anscombe, Oxford: Blackwell.

Wittgenstein, L. (1969), *On Certainty*, ed. G. E. M. Anscombe and G. H. von Wright, trans. D. Paul and G. E. M. Anscombe, Oxford: Blackwell.

Wolterstorff, N. (2001), *Thomas Reid and the Story of Epistemology*, Cambridge: Cambridge University Press.

Woolhouse, R. S. (1988), *The Empiricists*, Oxford: Oxford University Press.

Woudenberg, R. Van (2004), 'How to be a Common Sense Philosopher?', unpublished.

Wright, C. (1985), 'Facts and Certainty', *Proceedings of the British Academy* 71, 429–72.

Wright, C. (1991a), 'Scepticism and Dreaming: Imploding the Demon', *Mind* 397, 87–115.

Wright, C. (1991b), 'On Putnam's Proof That We Are Not Brains-in-a-Vat', *Proceedings of the Aristotelian Society* 92, 67–94.

Wright, C. (1992), *Truth and Objectivity*, Cambridge, MA: Harvard University Press.

Wright, C. (1993), *Realism, Meaning and Truth*, Oxford: Blackwell.

Wright, C. (2000), 'Cogency and Question-begging: Some Reflections on McKinsey's Paradox and Putnam's Proof', *Philosophical Issues* 10, 140–63.

Wright, C. (2003), 'Wittgensteinian Certainties', in McManus (2003), ch. 12.

Wright, C. (2004), 'Warrant for Nothing (and Foundations for Free)?', *Proceedings of the Aristotelian Society* 78 (supp. vol.), 167–212.

Zagzebski, L. (1993), *Rational Faith. Catholic Responses to Reformed Epistemology*, Notre Dame, IN: Notre Dame University Press.

Zagzebski, L. (1996), *Virtues of the Mind: An Inquiry into the Nature of Virtue and the Ethical Foundations of Knowledge*, Cambridge: Cambridge University Press.

Zagzebski, L. (2003), 'The Search for the Source of the Epistemic Good', in Brady and Pritchard (2003), 13–29.